やさしい英語を聴いて読む
IBCオーディオブックス

LEVEL
4
(2000-word)

グレート・ギャツビー
The Great Gatsby

F・スコット・フィッツジェラルド 原著

ニーナ・ウェグナー リライト

松澤喜好 監修

IBCパブリッシング

《使用語彙について》

レベル1：中学校で学習する単語約1000語
レベル2：レベル1の単語＋使用頻度の高い単語約300語
レベル3：レベル1の単語＋使用頻度の高い単語約600語
レベル4：レベル1の単語＋使用頻度の高い単語約1000語
レベル5：語彙制限なし

カバーデザイン

岩目地英樹 (コムデザイン)

ブックデザイン

鈴木一誌＋藤田美咲

ナレーション

Peter von Gomm

はじめに

英語の習得をめざす人が夢見るのは、「英語で感動することができる」レベルだと思います。「映画を字幕なしで見て感動したい」「海外ドラマを英語で楽しめるようになりたい」、そんな希望をお持ちのことでしょう。英語で感動し、そして他人をも感動させることができるようになれば、日本語と英語の両方で、人生を2倍楽しむことができてしまうのです。

英語が得意な日本人が最後まで苦しむのが、「リスニング100%」のレベルに到達することです。「リスニング100%」の状態とは、発音、語彙、文法、多読、多聴などで蓄積されたスキルが頭のなかで統合されている状態です。したがって、「リスニング100%」になることを目標にすえて学習することが英語マスターへの近道だと考えられます。しかし現状では、日本人がまとめて長時間の英語の音声を聴く機会は極端に少ないといえます。それに、ただ英語を1日中聴き流していれば目標に到達できるというわけでもありません。自分にあった教材を使用して、自分のレベルを上げていくプロセスを組み立ててこそ、「リスニング100%」の状態をものにすることができるのです。

これまでリスニングや発音の指導をしていて、リスニング学習へのアプローチを誤ったために伸び悩んでいる生徒にたくさん接してきました。彼らはそろってある典型的な誤りに陥っていたのです。これは最初に目標として定めたレベルに達するよりも早く、次の題材へと移ってしまうことに起因します。これではレベルアップの機会を自らつぶしていることになります。もっと分かりやすく説明しましょう。

● **Question**
　ここに1冊の日常英会話の練習用CDがあったとします。このCDの再生時間は60分間で、20章で構成されているとしましょう。あなたなら、このCDを使ってどのように練習しますか。以下の3とおりの方法を見てみましょう。

　　1章ずつ順番に1回ずつ声に出して発音しながら練習する。ひととおり終わったら、もう一度最初から20章を通して練習する。

……この方法では、一応1冊を終わらせてはいますが、発音やリスニングの練習としては、まったく不十分です。ではもう少し量を増やせばよいのでしょうか。

　　1章を5回くりかえしてから次の章に移る。20章まで同様にして、練習する。

……いわゆる勉強家のやりかたで、ご立派だと思います。この方法にはそれなりの勉強時間を確保する意志が必要だからです。その結果として少しは実力がつくと思われますが、発音やリスニングの練習方法としては、まだまだ不十分でレベルアップにはつながりません。

例3 ひととおり20章を最後まで聴いてから、一番好きな章をひとつだけ選ぶ。その章を携帯オーディオ機器にダウンロードして常に持ち歩き、50回から100回くりかえす。

……この方法なら、カタカナ式だった英語が、ようやく本来の英語に変身します。20章のうちのたったひとつの章をくりかえし聴けばよいので、例2と総合的な所要時間は一緒ですが、心理的な負担がぐっと軽くなります。

　なぜ例3の方法がもっとも有効なのかを、スポーツにたとえて説明しましょう。テニスでも野球でも、ラケットやバットの素振りをおこないます。素振りは、5回や10回では身につきません。数千回くりかえすことで、筋肉がつき、敏しょう性が備わり、やがて球を確実に返せるようになります。同様に、発音やリスニングも、カタカナ式発音から英語本来の発音へと変身するために必要な顔の筋肉、呼吸方法、確実性、敏しょう性を身につけるためには、数百回の練習が必要なのです。例2では、素振りの筋肉がつく前に次の練習に入ってしまっています。それに対して例3の方法なら、短い題材を何度もくりかえすことで、短時間のうちに急速に力がつくのです。

●オウムの法則

　ここまでで述べてきたことはParrot's Law「オウムの法則」に基づいています。これは私がオウムの調教にちなんで名づけた考えかたです。オウムは2,000回くりかえして初めてひとつの言葉を口にできるようになるといいます。たとえばまず「おはよう」ならそれを2,000回くりかえし教えます。ついに「おはよう」と言わせることに成功すれば、次にはたった200回の訓練で「こんばんは」が言えるようになります。英語学習もこれと同じで、早い段階で脳に英語の発音を刷

り込んでおくことが重要なのです。Parrot's Lawのねらいはそこにあります。日本人の英語学習法を見てみると、「おはよう」をマスターする前に「こんばんは」の練習に取りかかってしまうので、いつまでたってもひとことも話せないし、聴こえない状態に留まってしまうのです。オウムですら一生に一度、2,000回のくりかえしをするだけで言葉を発することを覚えます。鳥よりもはるかに学習能力が高い人間なら、100回もくりかえせば、カタカナ式発音をほんものの英語発音に変身させることができるはずです。

●短い英文を100回聴く

発音やリスニングが苦手な方は、まず短めの題材をひたすらくりかえし聴いて、英語の発音を完全に習得してしまいましょう。Parrot's Lawのメソッドなら、短い題材から大きな効果が期待できます。最初の50回までは、毎回少しずつ発見があり、自分の成長が実感できます。さすがに50回を超えると発音方法が分かるようになり、意味もほぼ理解して、英語で直接、場面をイメージできるようになります。同時に、自分の進歩が飽和してきて「これ以上は伸びないのでは？」と感じられます。でも実際には、50回を超えてからが肝心なのです。100回に向けて、脳に音の刷り込みをおこなっていきます。子音、母音、音節、イントネーション、複数の単語のかたまり、間の取りかた、息継ぎまでをそっくり再現できるまで練習しましょう。こうしてオウムでいうところの「おはよう」レベルに達することができるのです。

●仕上げの30分間

次にもう少し長めの20分から30分くらいの題材を聴いて、ストーリーを追ってみます。そしてそれを数十回くりかえし聴きます。これ

がParrot's Lawメソッドの仕上げ段階です。これにより、リスニングレベルは劇的に向上します。まったく未知のストーリーでも、英語で筋を追うことができるようになるのです。

　一生のうち一度、短い英文の朗読を100回くりかえして聴き、練習するだけで、発音とリスニングの壁を越えることができるのです。英語学習の早い時期に絶対に実施すべきトレーニングだと考えています。

● **オーディオブックス**
　アメリカでは、ベストセラーをオーディオブックスで楽しむスタイルが普及しています。ストーリーを味わいながら英語のリスニングスキルを伸ばしたいなら、オーディオブックスを聴いて想像力を働かせることがとても効果的です。しかしその一方で、ネイティブスピーカーを対象とした一般のオーディオブックスをいきなり聴いて挫折してしまう人がたくさんいることも事実です。日本の読者に向けた『IBCオーディオブックス』なら、楽しみながらParrot's Lawメソッドを実行することができます。『IBCオーディオブックス』のラインナップからお好きなものをチョイスして、挫折することなしにストーリーを楽しんでみてください。

『IBCオーディオブックス』活用法

　前述したようにアメリカでは、ベストセラーをオーディオブックスで楽しむスタイルが一般化しています。ストーリーを楽しみつつ英語のリスニングスキルを伸ばしたい人に、オーディオブックスはとても効果的だといえます。ところが、日本人英語学習者がいきなりネイティブスピーカー用のオーディオブックスを聴いても、スピードや語彙の問題から、挫折感を味わうだけとなってしまうかもしれません。英語初心者でも楽しみながら英語に親しめる『IBCオーディオブックス』は、いままでまとめて長時間の英語の音声に触れる機会がなかった日本の英語学習者に、初級から上級まで、幅広い音声を提供します。語彙のレベルや朗読のスピードが豊富なラインナップからお好みのタイトルを選び、上手に活用していただければ、リスニングをマスターすることが可能になります。

　では具体的に、『IBCオーディオブックス』を120％使いこなす方法を説明しましょう。

1　自分の心のままに「お気に入り」のトラックをみつける

　まず、『IBCオーディオブックス』のCD全体を、「テキストを見ずに」聴いてください。聴きかたは、音楽CDと同じ感覚でけっこうです。たとえば、買ったばかりの音楽CDを聴くときは、ひととおり聴いて、自分はどの曲が好きで、どの曲が嫌い、と心でチェックを入れています。『IBCオーディオブックス』のCDもまず全体を通して聴いてみて、自分の好きな曲＝トラックをみつけてみます。

聴いてみて内容が半分ぐらい理解できるようでしたら、テキストを見ないままで何度か続け、好きなトラックをみつけてください。ほとんど理解できない場合は、テキストを見ながら聴いて好きなトラックを選んでもかまいませんが、あくまでも基本は、「テキストを見ないで聴く」ことです。

　最初からほとんど聴き取れてしまった方は、次のステップ②へ進んでください。

　お気に入りのトラックをみつけたら、そこを何度もくりかえし聴いて、リスニングと朗読の練習をしましょう。Parrot's Lawのメソッドの第一歩、短いパートを100回くりかえす方法の実践です。くりかえし回数のめやすはだいたい以下のとおりですが、「自分が納得できるまで」を原則とします。100回より多くても少なくてもけっこうです。
　また、気に入ったトラックは携帯オーディオ機器に入れて持ち歩くと、空き時間をみつけてリスニング回数をかせぐことができますので、おすすめです。

- 30回程度、テキストを見ないで、ひたすらリスニングをおこなう。
- 次の30回は、テキストを見ながら、内容を理解する。
- 次の30回は、CDに続いて自分でも声を出して発音する。
- 次の10回で、テキストを見ないでリスニングが100％になった状態を確認する。

　これだけの練習を終えるころには、自分が選んだトラックについては、すべて理解できるようになっていることと思います。時間的には短いですが、練習の最後には、「リスニング100％」の状態を体験してみることが重要です。テキストを見ながら内容を理解している段階においては、積極的に辞書を引いて、発音もチェックしておい

てください。聴くだけでなく自分自身でも発音してみる次のステップに入るころには、文章をほぼ暗記できていると思います。

短めの1トラックを題材にして、じゅうぶんすぎるくらいに練習できたら、いよいよ、1冊全部を聴いてみてください。練習する前とくらべて驚くほど聴き取れるようになっている自分を発見するはずです。

2 リスニングと朗読の練習をする

ステップ①では、短めの1トラックだけに集中しましたが、このステップ②では、20分から30分程度の長めのリスニングをおこないます。ステップ①で選んだトラックを含む、前後20分程度のトラックを連続してくりかえし聴き、あわせて発音練習もします。全部で100回といいたいところですが、20回から30回でもじゅうぶんだと思います。聴きかたと練習法については、下記を参考にしてください。

- 10回程度、テキストを見ないで、ひたすらリスニングをおこなう。
- 次の10回は、テキストを見ながら、内容を理解する。
- 次の10回は、CDに続いて自分でも声を出して発音する。
- 次の5回で、テキストを見ないで、リスニングが100%になった状態を確認する。

3 ストーリーを楽しむ

以上の練習でリスニング力と正しい発音がしっかりと身についてきます。自分でもじゅうぶん練習したと納得できたら、本1冊分、トラック全部を通して聴いてみてください。練習を始める前とは見違えるように聴き取れると思います。リスニングでストーリーを追える自分に気づいて感動すると思います。この感動が、英語の学習を続ける大きなモチベーションになります。

英語でストーリーを楽しむという経験を味わうことによって、いままでの英語学習方法に変化が起きてきます。たとえば、子音・母音の発音方法についてもっと興味がわいてきて、真の発音練習ができるようになったりします。自身の語彙不足に気づいたり、これまで発音を正確に身につけていなかったことなどに気づくことで、辞書を引いたときにはその単語の発音までもチェックするようになります。いったんストーリーを楽しめるようになると、英語を語順のとおり直接理解していく習慣がつきます。英文をいちいち日本語に直したり、文末から後戻りしないと理解できないという状態が改善されます。洋書を読んでいても文章を単語の発音と結びつけられるようになります。聴くときも、読むときも、バラバラの単語単位ではなくて、複数の単語どうしのかたまりで意味をとらえていけるようになります。

　英会話や、英語でのプレゼンテーションにもよい影響が出始めます。発音の指導をしていると、「発音明快・意味不明」の人に出会います。発音はネイティブスピーカーレベルなのですが、目をつぶって聴いていても意味が伝わってこない人のことです。そうなってしまう最大の原因は、「伝える」ということを明確にイメージせずに、ただ英語を話しているところにあります。そうすると英語のイントネーションや、単語のかたまりごとのスピード調節、間の取りかたなどがないがしろにされてしまい、聴き手に意味が伝わらないのです。たとえネイティブスピーカーでも英単語をぶつ切りにして話をされれば、意味がわからなくなってしまうのです。ところが、リスニングによってストーリーを楽しめる段階までくれば、この「発音明快・意味不明」の状態は自然に改善されていきます。ストーリーを楽しめることは、ネイティブスピーカーの聴こえかたに近づいてくるからです。

4 『IBCオーディオブックス』のさきにあるもの

　自信がついてきたら、さらに『IBCオーディオブックス』からほかのタイトルを選んで楽しんでください。日本人の英語学習者は、そもそも英語に触れる絶対量が不足しているので、もっと積極的に英語に触れる機会をつくる必要があるのです。『IBCオーディオブックス』には難易度に合わせたレベル表示があるので、それを参考に、どんどんレベルの高いストーリーに進んでください。ただし、それを勉強としてとらえてしまってはいけません。楽しみながら実践した結果として大量の英語に触れている、というのが理想的です。英語に触れることを日常の習慣として取り入れることから始めるのです。

　そして、だんだんと実力がついてきたら、好きな映画やペーパーバック、海外のオーディオブックなども取り入れてみましょう。1日1時間としても、楽しみながら、1週間で7時間もの間、英語に触れていることが可能となります。それだけの時間、英語漬けといえる環境に身を置けば、英語を流しっぱなしにしているだけでも、どんどん実力がアップしていくでしょう。

　皆さんも『IBCオーディオブックス』で、英語を聴くことの楽しみを自分のものにしていってください。

- 本書のテキストは小社より刊行の「ラダーシリーズ」と共通です。
- 「あらすじ」のトラック番号は付属のCDに対応しています。2枚組のときは左がCD、右がトラックの番号となります。
- 本書のCDは、CDプレーヤーでご利用ください。パソコンのCDドライブなどでは正常に再生できない場合があります。

はじめに
3

『IBCオーディオブックス』活用法
8

あらすじ
15

Chapter 1
21

Chapter 2
31

Chapter 3
37

Chapter 4
47

Chapter 5
54

Chapter 6
63

Chapter 7
68

Chapter 8
78

Chapter 9
85

Chapter 10
97

Chapter 11
101

Chapter 12
107

Chapter 13
123

Chapter 14
133

Chapter 15
139

Chapter 16
145

Chapter 17
153

Word List
158

あらすじ | 15

TRACK 1-1
p.21~

Chapter 1
戦争から帰還した僕は、ニューヨーク郊外に小さな居を構えた。入江を挟んだ向こう側には、いとこのデイジーが富豪の夫トムと暮らしている。ある日二人を訪ねていくと、ジョーダンという若いプロゴルファーの女性を紹介され、四人で夕食をとった。トムの愛人の存在を知り、心乱された僕は帰宅後、夜空を見て気持ちを落ち着けていた。すると隣人のギャツビーらしき人影を見かける。彼は何を見ていたのだろう。（8分54秒）

キーワード
- [ ] criticize
- [ ] judge
- [ ] exception
- [ ] stockbroker
- [ ] mansion
- [ ] lawn
- [ ] butler
- [ ] rumor

TRACK 1-2
p.31~

Chapter 2
僕の住む地区とニューヨークの間には、巨大な眼鏡の看板の立つ、不気味な灰色の地帯がある。ある日の午後、僕はトムと車でニューヨークへ向かっていた。トムは灰色地帯にある車の修理工場へ立ち寄り、そこの主人ウィルソンに横柄に挨拶をした。そして彼の妻マートルに、夫の目を盗んで次の列車でニューヨークへ出てくるようにと指示をする。（4分53秒）

キーワード
- [ ] valley
- [ ] dust
- [ ] glasses
- [ ] advertisement
- [ ] affair
- [ ] repair
- [ ] complain
- [ ] dumb

TRACK 1-3
p.37~

Chapter 3
僕とトムは、トムの愛人マートルと同じ列車でニューヨークへ向かった。トムが借りているアパート最上階の部屋へ連れて行かれ、マートルの妹や近所の人々が集まり、ひどい酒盛りが始まった。マートルの妹は、僕の隣人ギャツビーの噂話を聞かせてくれた。トムが口論の末にマートルにけがを負わせるという騒ぎが起きて、僕はようやくその場を抜け出すことができた。（8分46秒）

キーワード
- [ ] puppy
- [ ] crowd
- [ ] fancy
- [ ] laughter
- [ ] servant
- [ ] introduction
- [ ] Catholic
- [ ] divorce

Chapter 4

TRACK 1-4
p.47~

隣人ギャツビーは毎週のようにパーティーを開いた。広大な敷地に飲み物、食べ物、電飾やテント、管弦楽団が用意され、通りには客の車がずらりと並んだ。誰でも自由に入り、何も気にせず楽しむことができた。僕は、招待してくれたギャツビーを探して会場を歩いていたが、彼を見つけることはできなかった。代わりに出会ったジョーダンと一緒にいると、常連客の娘からギャツビーに関する黒い噂を聞かされる。（5分59秒）

キーワード
- [ ] hire
- [ ] gardener
- [ ] orchestra
- [ ] invitation
- [ ] uncomfortable
- [ ] sure
- [ ] statement
- [ ] spy

Chapter 5

TRACK 1-5
p.54~

楽しく飲んでいると、同じテーブルの男からボートに誘われた。僕は相手が誰かも知らずに快諾したが、なんと彼がギャツビーだという。彼と別れてしばらくすると、ジョーダンがギャツビーに呼び出されて行ってしまい、僕は一人取り残された。パーティーが終わる頃に出てきたジョーダンは、話せないが、信じられないような話を聞いてきた、と言う。僕はギャツビーと改めてボートの約束をし、別れの挨拶をした。（7分18秒）

キーワード
- [ ] supper
- [ ] champagne
- [ ] army
- [ ] host
- [ ] I beg your pardon.
- [ ] old sport
- [ ] evil

Chapter 6

TRACK 1-6
p.63~

僕は普段は朝から真面目に仕事をし、夜は勉強や散歩をして過ごしている。プロゴルファーのジョーダンとは少しずつ仲良くなった。ある時、ささいな嘘をつく彼女を見て、彼女がかつてプレイ中の不正で新聞沙汰になったことを思い出す。彼女は不正直な人間だが、僕は彼女に愛着を感じてもいた。彼女も注意深い僕のことが好きだと言ってくれたが、正直者の僕は、故郷にいる女性のことが気にかかった。（3分27秒）

キーワード
- [ ] district
- [ ] tender
- [ ] curiosity
- [ ] cheat
- [ ] witness
- [ ] dishonest
- [ ] terrible
- [ ] careful

あらすじ | 17

Chapter 7

TRACK 1-7 p.68~

ある日、ギャツビーが訪ねてきて、彼と一緒にニューヨークへランチに出かけた。道中に彼が語った生い立ちはとても信じがたく思えたが、証拠の品や写真があるので本当らしかった。僕に何か頼みごとがあるが、それは後でジョーダンから聞いて欲しいというので、僕は少し不愉快に思った。レストランに着くと、ギャツビーの古い友人だという年配の男性を紹介される。彼が大物の賭博師だと知り唖然とする。
（8分42秒）

キーワード
- [ ] horn
- [ ] admire
- [ ] disappoint
- [ ] false
- [ ] wealthy
- [ ] award
- [ ] opportunity
- [ ] gamble

Chapter 8

TRACK 1-8 p.78~

その日の午後、僕はジョーダンからギャツビーの「頼みごと」と、それに付随する長い話を聞いた。5年前、いとこのデイジーとギャツビーは想い合っていた。デイジーはその後、トムと結婚したが。ギャツビーは、デイジーとの再会を期待してあの邸宅を買い、パーティーを開いていたのだ！ 彼の願いとは、僕の家にデイジーが遊びに来ているところへ、自分も顔を出させて欲しいというささやかなものだった。
（6分12秒）

キーワード
- [ ] officer
- [ ] Red Cross
- [ ] engage
- [ ] string
- [ ] run into
- [ ] arrange
- [ ] suppose

Chapter 9

TRACK 1-9 p.85~

デイジーを招待する打ち合わせ中、ギャツビーは神経質なほど万事に気を遣った。約束の日は雨で、ギャツビーの顔は青白く、ひどく不安げだった。ついに再会した二人は、最初こそ緊張して気まずそうだったが、しばらく二人きりにすると、すっかり幸せそうに見つめ合っていた。ギャツビーはデイジー（と僕）に豪邸を案内して見せた。ギャツビーの5年間を思いながら、僕はそっとその場を離れ、歩いて家に戻った。
（10分40秒）

キーワード
- [ ] pale
- [ ] anxious
- [ ] calm down
- [ ] stiff
- [ ] excuse
- [ ] embarrass
- [ ] law
- [ ] puzzle

18 | あらすじ

TRACK 2-1 p.97~

Chapter 10
ずいぶん後になって、ギャツビーが教えてくれた話だ。彼の本名はジェイムズ・ギャッツ。彼は16歳の頃に豊かな暮らしに憧れて家を出て、名を変えた。あるとき大金持ちのダン・コーディーに出会い、気に入られて雇われの身になった。二人で世界中を旅して、それが5年続いたある日、コーディーが亡くなった。ギャツビーに遺された金は、コーディーの妻の画策によって手に入ることはなかったという。
(2分48秒)

キーワード
- [ ] farm
- [ ] accept
- [ ] yacht
- [ ] storm
- [ ] row
- [ ] seek
- [ ] independent

TRACK 2-2 p.101~

Chapter 11
ギャツビーとトムは、ふとしたことからついに顔見知りになり、ギャツビー邸のパーティーにトムとデイジーが参加する日が訪れた。パーティーの豪華さと出席者の顔ぶれにトムは驚いた。デイジーはパーティーを楽しまず、ギャツビーは落胆する。僕は、ギャツビーがデイジーに対して何を望んでいるのかがわかった。僕はギャツビーに「過去は繰り返せない」と言ったが、彼はそうは思っていないようだった。
(5分00秒)

キーワード
- [ ] by accident
- [ ] delight
- [ ] politician
- [ ] taste
- [ ] gangster
- [ ] marriage
- [ ] apart

TRACK 2-3 p.107~

Chapter 12
ある暑い日、昼食会の席で、トムはデイジーとギャツビーが通じ合っていることに気づき、そのことを僕たちも察した。おかしな雰囲気のまま、全員で街へ出かけた。給油に立ち寄った修理工場の主人も、妻の浮気に感づいていた。暑さに苛立ち、ついにトムはギャツビーの糾弾を始める。デイジーはギャツビーへの愛を口にするが、トムの問いかけに反論できない。さらにトムはギャツビーの黒い噂を暴露していく。
(14分59秒)

キーワード
- [ ] fire
- [ ] demand
- [ ] cool
- [ ] speed off
- [ ] gas
- [ ] afford
- [ ] remark
- [ ] cause

あらすじ | 19

TRACK 2-4
p.123~

Chapter 13
僕とトムとジョーダンは、帰る途中、修理工場の夫人マートルがひき逃げに遭い、殺されたことを知った。ひいたのはギャツビーの車であることを僕らは知った。戻ってくるとトムの家の近くで、ギャツビーが闇に紛れて立っていた。車を運転していたのはデイジーだという。ギャツビーはデイジーがトムに乱暴されないか監視していると言ったが、僕の目には、デイジーとトムには夫婦の結びつきがあるように見えた。
(8分57秒)

キーワード
☐ Greek ☐ yell ☐ lock ☐ bend
☐ rock ☐ footstep ☐ wheel

TRACK 2-5
p.133~

Chapter 14
明け方、ギャツビーが帰ってくる音がして、僕は出かけて行った。僕は彼にここを離れるように言ったが、聞き入れられそうもなかった。彼から、ダン・コーディーの話や、デイジーとの思い出話を聞いた。朝食の後、一緒にプールで泳がないかと誘われたが、僕は仕事へ行く時間が迫っていた。僕はギャツビーに賛美の言葉と、朝食のお礼を言って、仕事へ向かった。(5分01秒)

キーワード
☐ dawn ☐ ought to ☐ station ☐ reassuring
☐ fortune ☐ praise ☐ bear to

TRACK 2-6
p.139~

Chapter 15
僕はその日は仕事にならず、早退した。僕は自分が現場を去ってからのことを後で知ることになる。妻を殺されたウィルソンは、殺したやつを絶対に見つけ出してみせると決意し、姿を消していた。僕がギャツビーの家にかけつけたとき、プールの真ん中には血を流したギャツビーが浮かび、少し離れた芝生に自殺したウィルソンの死体があった。
(5分19秒)

キーワード
☐ line ☐ see if ☐ drawer ☐ leash
☐ trick ☐ trace ☐ grass

20 | あらすじ

TRACK 2-7
p.145~

Chapter 16
ギャツビーの死を気にかけている人間は僕しかいないようだった。デイジーとトムは大量の荷物とともに姿を消した。ようやく彼の父親と連絡がつき、痩せて打ちひしがれた老人が現れた。ギャツビーに商売のすべてを教えたという賭博師の男は、警察にマークされるから葬儀には出られないという。雨の中で行われた葬儀に参列したのは、僕と、彼の父親と、使用人たちだけだった。(7分19秒)

キーワード
- [ ] delay
- [ ] funeral
- [ ] position
- [ ] mix up in
- [ ] generous
- [ ] minister
- [ ] bury

TRACK 2-8
p.153~

Chapter 17
僕は東部ニューヨークでの暮らしには馴染めないと思い、西部に戻ることにした。ジョーダンとの関係は終わった。トムに偶然会った時、ウィルソンにギャツビーのことを教えたのはトムだったことと、デイジーは自分がひき逃げ犯であることをトムにも言っていないことを知った。僕は2人がぞんざいな人間だということを悟った。東部での最後の夜、僕はギャツビーの家を眺め、彼と、彼の夢について思いを馳せた。(3分49秒)

キーワード
- [ ] West
- [ ] East
- [ ] suitable
- [ ] criminal
- [ ] deserve
- [ ] suffer
- [ ] sand
- [ ] reach forward

Chapter 1

When I was younger, my father gave me some advice that I never forgot. He said to me, "If you ever feel like criticizing anyone, just remember that not everybody has had the advantages you have had." That was all he said, but it was enough for me to understand. I took that advice seriously. So, all my life I have listened to people without judging them. Many people realized I was a good listener and told me all about their problems—even things I didn't want to hear about. Finally, after hearing so many people's deepest, darkest secrets, there came a point when I didn't want to listen to other people anymore. I wanted to be left alone.

Gatsby, who I named this book after, was the only exception. Gatsby was one of the most interesting people I ever met. He was full of hopes and dreams. I respected that, even though I didn't agree with most of the things he did.

I come from a family of successful businessmen. They all live in the Midwest. I went to college in New Haven, then I joined the army to fight in WWI. When I returned to America, I felt bored and useless, so I decided to become a New York stockbroker. Everyone was becoming a stockbroker in those days, so I thought I would do it too. I moved out to the East Coast in 1922.

I decided to live in a little house on Long Island, in the countryside just outside of New York City. I took the train to the office everyday. My house was located where two hills that look like huge eggs stuck out into the bay. They were called West Egg and East Egg. The two pieces of land were shaped exactly alike, but the lives led on each egg were very different.

I lived at West Egg, which was the less fashionable of the two. My little house was built in between two huge mansions. The one on my right was the bigger mansion, with a swimming pool and a lawn that seemed to go on forever. That was Gatsby's house. I didn't know Gatsby at the time, but I knew a man named Gatsby lived there. Across the bay at East Egg lived my cousin Daisy and her husband Tom. Tom was known as one of the best football players of his time when he was in college at New Haven. He came from a very rich family. He often spent money in a way that shocked people.

Tom and Daisy were so rich they could do whatever they wanted. They even lived in France for a year. But they came back to America and just floated around here and there. Daisy said now they planned to stay in East Egg forever, but I didn't believe her. It seemed to me that Tom would continue to float around, searching for the same kind of excitement he had in his old football days.

One evening soon after I moved to West Egg, I went to visit Daisy and Tom. Their house was bigger and more cheerful than I expected. It looked over the bay and had a huge lawn that ran straight down to the beach. That evening, the sunset had turned all the front windows gold, and Tom was standing on the porch in his horse-riding clothes.

Tom had changed since his college days. Now he was a man of thirty, with a hard mouth and a proud manner. His clothes could not seem to contain the power of his large body. When he moved, you could see his muscles under his thin coat. It was a body that could do great harm. It was a cruel body. Tom made people feel small, and many of his classmates at college had disliked him. But for some reason, Tom had always liked me.

We talked on the porch before going into the house.

"I've got a nice place here," Tom said. His eyes flashed around the grounds from here to there. Then he led me inside.

We went into the living room, where we met Daisy and another young lady seated on a couch. Both women were dressed in white and looked so pretty and light. Daisy laughed when she saw me. I laughed too.

"I'm so happy to see you!" said Daisy. "This is my friend Miss Baker."

The other young woman just nodded at me. She looked familiar, and I realized she was Jordan Baker, a famous professional golf player. Daisy looked up at me as if there were no other person in the world she would rather see. That was a way she had. She started to ask me questions in her lovely voice. It was a voice that you could follow like a strange piece of music. She had bright eyes and a bright mouth, and her face was both beautiful and sad.

I looked at Jordan again and suddenly I remembered that I had heard some story about her. It was something in the newspapers—something unpleasant—but it was a long time ago and I couldn't remember what it was.

"What are you doing these days, Nick?" Tom asked.

"I sell stocks," I said.

"Don't you live in West Egg?" Jordan asked. "I know somebody who lives there. You must know him too, his name is Gatsby."

"Gatsby?" asked Daisy. "Who is Gatsby?"

Before I could reply that he was my neighbor, the dinner bell rang, and we all moved to the table that was set outside.

We sat down to eat and talked about this and that. Tom started to talk about a book he had read called "The Rise of the Colored Empires." He said it was important for us as white people to read it. He explained that science proved that the white race was the best and strongest race in the world, and we needed to watch out for other races that were trying to take over.

"We've got to beat those other races down," said Daisy. She winked at me, and I knew she was making fun of Tom.

Tom began to argue his point again when he was cut off by the loud ring of the telephone. The butler came out and whispered something into Tom's ear. Tom got up and went inside. After Tom had been gone a minute, Daisy stood up and went inside too. I did not think anything was the matter and started to say something to Jordan Baker. But she held up her hand and stopped me.

"Sh!" she said. "I want to hear what's going on." Then she leaned forward, listening to the faint voices coming from inside the house.

"Is something wrong?" I asked, surprised

that Jordan didn't feel any shame in listening to other peoples' private conversations.

"You mean you don't know?" she asked. "I thought everybody knew."

"Knew what?"

"Tom has some woman in New York."

"Some woman?"

"I can't believe she would call him in the middle of dinner!" Jordan said. But Daisy and Tom returned to the table, and Jordan dropped the subject.

After dinner, we all sat in the living room again. Jordan read out loud to us from *The Saturday Evening Post,* and at ten o'clock, she went to bed. Daisy, Tom, and I were left together.

"She's a nice girl," said Tom.

"Yes. In fact, I think I shall make you marry her, Nick," said Daisy. "She's staying with us most of the summer and you'll see her often. I'll make sure you two fall in love and marry." She laughed her charming little laugh, and I knew she was not serious about any of it.

"Nick, weren't you engaged to marry a girl out West?" asked Tom.

"No, that's not true. That's all rumors," I said.

Soon I got up to leave and headed home. As I drove back to West Egg, I felt confused and upset about what I had seen at Daisy and Tom's house. Tom was having an affair that everyone knew about. I thought Daisy should leave Tom forever. But Daisy did not seem to think that was necessary at all.

When I got home, I decided to sit outside for a while and look at the night sky. I was relaxing like this when I noticed a shadow about fifty feet away from me. A man stood with his hands in his pockets, looking across the bay. I realized it was probably my neighbor Gatsby. I was going to call out to him, but he suddenly stretched his arms out toward the bay, and it looked to me like his body was shaking a little. I looked toward the bay to see what he was looking at, but I only saw a single green light, like something at the end of a dock. When I looked once more for Gatsby, he was gone, and I was alone in the darkness.

Chapter 2

TRACK 1-2 Between West Egg and New York is a sad-looking gray bit of land. It is a valley of dust, like some farm in a sad dream where dust grows like grain. Dust takes the shape of hills, houses, and even men who move like gray ghosts through the dust-filled air. Sometimes a line of train cars pulls up in the valley and comes to a slow stop. Then the gray ghost men pick up their shovels and dig into the train cars, stirring up a great cloud of even more gray dust.

But high above the gray land stands a great sight: the eyes of Doctor T. J. Eckleburg.

The eyes of Doctor T. J. Eckleburg are blue and huge. Just the colored parts of the eyes are three feet high. The eyes are not a part of a face. They just stare out of a huge pair of yellow eye glasses. Some crazy eye doctor paid for this advertisement to be put there, in the land of dust, to increase his business. At some point he must have forgotten about it or moved away. But the eyes remained there, watching over the gray land with their yellow glasses.

This unpleasant scene is where I met Tom's woman one day. Everyone knew that Tom was having an affair. Although I was curious about the woman, I had no desire to meet her. But one afternoon, as Tom and I drove into New York City for the day, Tom insisted on stopping. We were driving through the valley of dust when Tom said, "We're stopping here. I want you to meet my girl."

He pulled the car off the road and stopped it. We got out and I followed him across a dusty yard, under the huge staring eyes of Doctor Eckleburg. The only building in sight was a small block of yellow brick sitting on the edge of a little street. One of its three shops was a car repair shop. A sign in front read, "Repairs. George B. Wilson. Cars bought and sold." I followed Tom inside.

The inside of the shop was small and bare. The owner of the shop was clearly poor. The only car in the place was a broken old truck in a dark corner. Then the owner of the shop appeared from the office door. He was a thin man with light-colored hair. He looked very tired. He was wiping his dirty hands on a piece of cloth. When he saw Tom, a look of weak hope lit up in his eyes.

"Hello, Wilson," said Tom. He slapped the thin man cheerfully on the shoulder and asked, "How's business?"

"I can't complain," Wilson said. It looked to me like there was plenty for Wilson to complain about.

"When are you going to sell me your car?" he asked Tom.

"Next week," replied Tom. "My man is working on it now."

"Seems like he works pretty slow," said Wilson. This angered Tom.

"No he doesn't," he replied coldly. "And if you feel that way about it, maybe I should sell it to somebody else."

Wilson looked scared.

"Oh, I don't mean to make trouble," said Wilson quickly. "I just mean—"

But his voice trailed off and Tom looked around the garage. We heard footsteps on the stairs, and in a moment the thick shape of a woman blocked the light coming from the office door. She was in her mid-thirties and was rather large, but she carried her extra weight pleasantly as some women can. Her face was not beautiful, but there was a visible air of life and excitement about her, as if her blood was always running hot.

She smiled slowly and walked past her husband toward Tom. She shook hands with Tom, looking straight into his eyes. She did not look at her husband as she said, "Go get some chairs, George, so these people can sit down."

"Oh, sure," said George. He hurried away to find some. When he was gone, the woman moved closer to Tom.

"I want to see you," Tom said. "Get on the next train."

"All right."

"I'll meet you by the newspaper stand on the lower level of the station," Tom said.

She nodded and moved away from him just as George entered the room with two chairs. Tom and I left. We drove to the nearest station and waited for her get on the train. A little child played in the gray dust on the side of the street.

"Terrible place, isn't it?" Tom said. He looked uneasily at Doctor Eckleburg.

"It's awful."

"It's good for her to get away from here," he said.

"What about her husband? Doesn't he say anything?"

"Wilson? He thinks she goes to see her sister in New York. He's so dumb he doesn't know he's alive."

Chapter 3

So it came to be that Tom, his girl, and I went together to New York. Well, sort of together. Tom and I rode in a different train car from his girl so that nobody would see us riding all together. At the train station in New York, we met his girl. Tom helped her down from the train. At a store in the station, she bought herself a magazine, some face cream, and a bottle of perfume. Once outside, she chose a new, purple-colored taxi for us to ride in. But as soon as we got into the taxi, she knocked on the driver's window to make him stop.

"I want to buy one of those dogs there,"

she said, pointing to a man standing on the street, selling puppies out of a basket. "A dog is nice to have in the apartment."

The driver stopped and Tom bought her a dog. Mrs. Wilson pet it happily while it sat in her lap.

When we drove up to Fifth Avenue, I finally said I had to go. I tried to stop the car and get out, but Tom wouldn't let me.

"Myrtle will be hurt if you don't come up to see the apartment. Won't you Myrtle?" Tom said.

"Come on," she said to me. "I'll have my sister come over too, and lots of people say she's very beautiful."

"Well, I'd really like to—" I began, but nobody listened to me and the taxi drove on.

We arrived at the apartment on 158th Street. As we got out of the taxi, Mrs. Wilson looked around the street as if she owned it. She gathered her bags and went into the white apartment building with her nose high in the air.

"I'm going to invite the McKees to come over," she announced, as we went upstairs. "And of course, I'll call up my sister, too."

The apartment was on the top floor. It had a small living room, a small dining room, a small bedroom, and a bath. The living room was so crowded with big furniture that it was difficult to move around the room. There were several old magazines about movie stars and famous people on the table. The only picture in the room was a bad photo of a hen sitting on a rock. But I discovered that if you walked far enough away from the picture and looked at it again, the hen was actually a hat and the rock was actually the face of an old woman.

Mrs. Wilson found a box and some milk for the dog. Tom brought out a bottle of whiskey from a locked closet.

I have only been drunk twice in my life. The second time was that afternoon, so everything that happened has a dreamy feel to it. At one point I went out to buy some cigarettes, and when I came back, Tom and Mrs. Wilson had disappeared. I sat waiting quietly in the living room until they appeared again a while later. By that time, I had already finished my first drink.

People began to arrive at the apartment. Catherine, Myrtle's sister, was a tall, thin girl of about thirty. She had a solid, sticky mass of red hair. The powder on her face made her skin milky white. Mr. McKee was a neighbor from downstairs. He was a small man who said he was a photographer. I found out later that it was him who had taken the picture of the old woman on the wall. The old woman was Myrtle's mother.

Although Mr. McKee's wife was pretty, she was loud and awful. She told me with pride that her husband had photographed her one-hundred and twenty-seven times since they had been married.

Myrtle had changed her clothes a little

earlier. Now she wore a fancy, cream-colored dress that made noises every time she moved. Along with her dress, her attitude seemed to change too. Her voice, her movements, and her laughter all took on an air of loud and rough pride. As she grew louder, the room seemed to grow smaller around her.

"I like your dress," Mrs. McKee said. "It's so pretty."

Myrtle brushed aside the praise right away.

"Oh, this? It's just a crazy old dress," she said, her nose held high in the air. "I only wear it when I don't care what I look like."

Tom yawned and stood up. "You McKees should have another drink," he said. "Myrtle, get some more ice for the drinks before everybody falls asleep."

"I told that servant boy to bring us some ice," said Myrtle. "These people! You have to stay on top of them all the time!" She looked at me and laughed as if I was agreeing with her every word. Then she picked up the dog and gave it a kiss. Then she got up and walked into the kitchen making extra noises with her dress, as if she had a dozen cooks waiting for her orders in there.

Her sister, Catherine, came and sat down next to me.

"Do you live down on Long Island too?" she asked.

"I live at West Egg," I replied.

"Really? I was at a party there about a month ago," she said, "at a man named Gatsby's. Do you know him?"

"I live next door to him."

"Well they say he's related to some German king, Kaiser Wilhelm or something," she said. "That's where all his money comes from."

Mr. McKee was speaking to Tom then, and I heard him saying that he would like to take more photos on Long Island.

"All I need is an introduction to get me started there," Mr. McKee was saying.

"Ask Myrtle," said Tom with a loud shout

of laughter. "She'll write you a grand letter of introduction. You can photograph her husband and call it 'George Wilson Selling Gas,' or something." Tom roared with laughter.

Catherine leaned over and whispered to me, "Neither Tom nor Myrtle like the person they're married to."

"No?" I asked.

"No, they can't stand them. I think they should both get divorced and marry each other right away. But Tom's wife won't let him. She's Catholic and doesn't believe in divorce."

This was interesting because I knew Daisy wasn't Catholic. I was shocked at how deep Tom's lies went.

"Why did you ever marry George Wilson, Myrtle? You don't even like him, and nobody forced you to," Catherine said. Myrtle thought for a while.

"I married him because I thought he was a gentleman," she finally said. "But after I married him I knew it was a mistake. He had to borrow somebody's best suit to wear to our wedding. When I found that out, I cried all day long."

"She really ought to get away from him," Catherine said to me. "They've been living above that garage for eleven years and Tom is the first lover Myrtle has ever had."

The second bottle of whiskey got passed around. I wanted to get out and walk toward Central Park into the soft darkness of the night. But every time I tried to go, I would get caught up in some wild argument that pulled me back into my chair.

Suddenly, Myrtle was sitting very close to me and telling me about when she first met Tom.

"We were sitting in the same train car to New York," she said, her warm breath pouring over me. "He had on a nice suit and shoes. I couldn't keep my eyes off of him, and every time he looked at me I had to look away quickly. When we got off at the station, he pressed the front of his shirt to my arm and I told him I would have to call the police. But he knew I lied. I was so excited when I got into a taxi with him. All I kept thinking, over and over, was 'You can't live forever; you can't live forever.'"

It was nine o'clock. Then suddenly it was ten o'clock. Mr. McKee was asleep on a chair. The dog was sitting on the table trying to see through the cigarette smoke. People disappeared, then appeared again. They made plans to go somewhere, then lost each other, searched for each other, and found each other a few feet away. Some time around midnight, Tom and Myrtle stood face to face, arguing. The argument was about whether Myrtle had any right to say Daisy's name.

"Daisy! Daisy! Daisy!" shouted Myrtle. "I'll say it whenever I want! Daisy! Dai—"

Suddenly Tom reached out and hit her with his open hand, breaking her nose.

Then there were bloody towels on the bathroom floor, and women's voices accusing Tom, and over it all, cries of pain. Mr. McKee woke up and looked at the scene around him. He took his hat and walked out the door. I followed him. Then I was lying half asleep on the cold lower level of Pennsylvania Station, waiting for the four o'clock train.

Chapter 4

Music came from my neighbor's house through the summer nights. In the afternoons, I would see his guests swimming in the ocean or lying on his beach. All day, his two motor-boats full of people would race across the blue waters, leaving long white trails behind them. On the weekends, his Rolls Royce became a bus that brought people to and from the city between nine in the morning and long past midnight. And on Mondays, eight servants and a gardener would work all day cleaning up the damage from the night before.

Every Friday, five wooden boxes of oranges and lemons came from a fruit shop in New York City. Every Monday, these same oranges and lemons left Gatsby's back door in a mountain of peels. There was a machine in the kitchen that could remove the juice from two hundred oranges in half an hour if somebody pressed a little button two hundred times.

Every ten days or so, a group of hired help came with several hundred feet of white cloth and colored lights to make party tents in Gatsby's huge garden. Baked hams, chickens, salads, and fruits were arranged on long tables. There were so many different kinds of liquor in the bar that just the sight of them made you feel drunk.

By seven o'clock, the musicians would arrive—not some little five-piece band, but a full orchestra. By this time, the last swimmers would be back and dressing upstairs. There would be cars from New York parked all along the street, and already the halls and rooms would be full of bright colors and women with stylish haircuts. The bar would be busy, and waiters would be serving drinks in the garden. The air would come alive with voices and laughter. Women who never knew each other's names would greet each other warmly.

As the hour gets later and later, laughter spills out more easily. The lights burn brighter, and the groups of people change more quickly. They grow bigger with new arrivals and shrink as people float over to the next group. Confident girls move alone through groups of men, saying something clever and becoming the center of attention for a brief moment. Then they move on to the next group.

At some point in the night, a girl grabs a drink out of thin air, drinks it down, and steps out onto the dance floor. The music changes to something a little faster, and she begins to dance all by herself. As more people join her, the party has really begun.

I believe that on the first night I went to Gatsby's house, I was one of the few people who were actually invited. Most people who came to the parties weren't really invited—they didn't need to be. They simply got into cars, made their way to Long Island, and showed up at Gatsby's door. They were never turned away. Some were introduced to Gatsby by somebody else who knew him, but some came and stayed the whole night without ever meeting Gatsby at all. And that seemed to be just fine.

Gatsby had actually sent his servant, dressed in a light-blue uniform, to my house to deliver an invitation. The card he handed to me said that Gatsby would be honored if I could attend his "little party" that night. It also said Gatsby had seen me several times before but never had a chance to meet me. It was signed "Jay Gatsby" in fancy writing.

I put on my nice white suit and went over to his house a little after seven o'clock. I felt a little uncomfortable as I walked among groups of people I didn't know. I tried to find Gatsby as soon as I arrived to thank him for inviting me. But, try as I might, I could not find him anywhere. Feeling unhappy, I walked over to the bar and stayed there for a long time. It was the only place I could stay without looking so useless and alone.

I was on my way to getting very drunk when I saw Jordan Baker enter the garden. She stood on the steps leading from the house to the garden.

"Hello!" I shouted as I made my way toward her.

"I thought I'd see you here," she said. She rested her golden arm on mine, and we walked through the garden together. We sat down at a table where two girls dressed in yellow were sitting with three gentlemen.

"Do you come to these parties often?"

Jordan asked the girl beside her.

"Sure," said the girl. "I like to come. I never care what I do here, so I always have a good time. When I was here last I tore my dress on a chair. Gatsby asked me my name and address and in one week I got a package with a new dress in it."

"Did you keep it?" asked Jordan.

"Sure I did," said the girl. "I was going to wear it tonight, but it was a little too big and had to be fixed. It was gas blue with purple beads. Two hundred and sixty-five dollars."

"There's something strange about a man who will do a thing like that," said the other girl. "He doesn't want trouble with anybody. Somebody told me—" the two girls and Jordan leaned in toward each other and spoke in quiet voices.

"Somebody told me they thought he killed a man once." The statement got us all excited. The three men leaned forward to hear.

"No, I heard he was a German spy during

the war," said the other girl. One of the men nodded in agreement.

"I heard that from a man who knew all about him, and even grew up with him in Germany," the man said.

"Oh, no," said the first girl, "that can't be, because he was in the American army during the war." Now we all believed her instead of the other man, and she added, "Just look at him sometimes when he thinks nobody is looking. I bet he killed a man."

We all turned to look for Gatsby, but of course he was nowhere to be found.

Chapter 5

After supper, Jordan and I tried to find Gatsby. First, we went to the bar, but he was not there. Then we went to the top of the stairs to look down onto the garden, but she couldn't see him. We wandered into a very large, old-fashioned library, but he wasn't there either.

When we went back outside, people were dancing in the garden. By midnight, everyone was drunk and laughing. A few famous singers at the party had sang some songs, the champagne was being served in glasses that were the size of bowls, and the moon had risen higher. Jordan was still with me. We sat at a table with a man of about my age and a loud young girl who laughed at everything. After all the champagne, I was feeling very happy.

During a pause in all the talking and laughing, the man looked at me and said politely, "Your face is familiar to me. Were you in the Third Division during the war?"

"Why, yes, I was."

"I was in the army until June of 1918. I knew I had seen you somewhere before."

We talked for a moment about some little villages in France. Then he told me he had just bought a new motor-boat and invited me to take it out on the water with him the next morning.

"Sure, what time?" I said.

"Any time you like."

I was just about to ask the man his name when Jordan turned around and said to me, "Are you having a good time now?"

"Much better now," I said, and turned back to the man.

"This is an unusual party for me," I said. "I haven't even seen the host. I live over there—" I waved my hand toward my house across the lawn, "and this man Gatsby sent his servant over to invite me."

For a moment he looked at me as if he didn't understand.

"I'm Gatsby," he said suddenly.

"What! Oh, I beg your pardon."

"I thought you knew, old sport. I'm afraid I'm not a very good host," said Gatsby. Then he gave me a smile that was full of understanding and warmth. It was one of those precious smiles that seemed to reassure you about everything you've ever done in your life. It saw you as you hoped others would see you, it believed in you as you would like to believe in yourself, it respected who you were. But just as I saw all this, the smile disappeared, and I was just looking at a fashionable young man.

Just then, a servant hurried over to Gatsby and said somebody from Chicago was calling on the phone. Gatsby bowed to all of us and excused himself. Before he left, he turned to me and said, "If you want anything just ask for it, old sport. Excuse me. I will join you again later."

When he was gone I turned to Jordan. He was not anything like I expected. For some reason I had thought Gatsby would be a rather fat man in middle age.

"Who is he?" I asked. "Do you know?"

"He's just a man named Gatsby," said Jordan.

"Yes, I know, but where is he from, I mean? And what does he do?"

"Oh, now *you're* curious about it," she answered with a smile. "Well, he told me once that he went to Oxford for college. But I don't believe it."

"Why not?"

"I don't know. I just don't think he went

there," she said. "Anyway, he gives large parties. I like large parties."

Later in the night, as I was listening to the music and watching different people dance, my eyes fell on Gatsby, standing alone on the grand steps. He looked from one group to another, watching everyone. He was handsome, and his short hair looked like it was cut perfectly every day. I could see nothing evil or bad in him, as others seemed to. I wondered if the fact that he did not drink separated him from his guests. The more his guests drank and laughed, the more correct and wise Gatsby seemed to me.

When a slow song started, girls put their heads on men's shoulders, and couples danced slowly. But no girl put her head on Gatsby's shoulder. No one danced with him.

"I beg your pardon." One of Gatsby's servants was standing next to us and speaking to Jordan.

"Are you Miss Baker?" he asked. "Mr.

Gatsby would like to speak to you alone."

"With me?" Jordan asked with surprise.

"Yes, Miss."

She got up slowly, looking at me with large, surprised eyes. She followed the man into the house. Then I was alone, and it was almost two o'clock in the morning. I decided to move inside. A large room was full of people. One of the girls in yellow was playing the piano, and singing beside her was a tall, red-haired young lady from a famous theater group. She had had a lot of champagne, and during her song she had decided that everything was very, very sad. She was not only singing, but weeping too. Her tears rolled down her cheeks, making black trails down her face.

"She had a fight with a man who says he's her husband," explained a girl standing near me.

I looked around. Most of the remaining women were now having fights with their husbands. In the hall were two couples. The two men were not drunk at all, and the two women were angry. The women spoke to each other in raised voices.

"Whenever he sees I'm having a good time, he wants to go home," one said.

"I never heard of anything so selfish in my life," the other said.

"We're always the first ones to leave."

"So are we."

"Well, we're one of the last to leave tonight," said one of the men in a small voice. "The orchestra left half an hour ago."

After a bit more arguing, the night ended for both couples with the men picking up their wives and carrying them out the door. The women kicked, but they all disappeared into the night.

As I waited for my hat in the hall, the door of the library opened and Jordan and Gatsby came out together. He was saying some last words to her, but he saw some of his guests leaving and started to say goodbye.

Jordan came over to me and shook my hand.

"I've just heard the most unbelievable thing," she whispered. "How long were we in there?"

"About an hour," I told her.

"It was...unbelievable," she repeated. "But I swore I wouldn't tell anyone about it." She yawned. She seemed tired. "Please come and see me some time...Goodbye." She joined the party of people she had come with and walked out the door.

I stepped toward Gatsby to say goodbye and to apologize for not knowing him in the garden earlier.

"Don't worry about it, old sport," said Gatsby, shaking my hand. "Don't give it another thought. And don't forget we're going out in my boat tomorrow morning."

Then one of his servants said behind Gatsby's shoulder, "Somebody in Philadelphia is calling you on the phone, sir."

"All right, tell them I'll be there in a minute," Gatsby replied. Then to me he said, "Good night, old sport. Good night."

Chapter 6

After reading over everything I have written, I realize that it sounds like parties were all that I cared about. That's not true. Actually, I was very busy that summer, and what took up most of my time was work. In the early morning, I hurried down the streets of New York City to the business district. I would work all day and go to lunch with other men my age. I usually had dinner at the Yale Club, and then I went upstairs to the library and studied stocks for about an hour. After that, if it was a nice night, I would go for a walk down Madison Avenue.

I began to like New York. It felt fast and busy and always full of people. There was adventure everywhere. But sometimes, later at night as I walked through the streets, I felt a sinking feeling of loneliness. And I could tell others felt it too—sometimes I saw other young working men walking all alone to dinner. I knew they felt as lonely as me.

I didn't hear from Jordan Baker for a while. But in the middle of summer, we connected again. At first I felt lucky to be able to go places with her, because she was a famous golfer and everyone knew her name. But then this feeling turned into something more. It was not love, but I felt a tender curiosity toward her. The bored, proud look on her face seemed to hide something, and I wondered about it. One day, I found out what it was.

We were at a party at somebody's house. Jordan borrowed somebody's car and left it out in the rain with the top down, and then she lied about it. Suddenly I remembered the unpleasant story about Jordan that I could not remember the first night I met her at Daisy's house. Jordan had cheated in her first golf tournament. It was such a big deal that the story made it into the newspapers. People said that she had moved her ball from a bad spot on the course. But then the witnesses took back their statements, and everybody forgot the whole thing.

Jordan was a dishonest person, and that's what she was hiding from the world. But I didn't care. And sooner or later, I forgot about it.

The evening we were coming home from the house party where Jordan had lied about the car, she drove me home. She was a bad driver, and she almost hit a person on the street.

"You're a terrible driver," I said to her. "You should either be more careful or not drive at all."

"I am careful," she said.

"No, you're not."

"Well, other people are," she said lightly.

"What does that have to do with it?"

"They will keep out of my way," she said. "It takes two people to make an accident."

"What if you met somebody as careless as yourself?"

"I hope I never will," she answered. "I don't like careless people. That's why I like you."

It was one of the first tender things Jordan had ever said to me, and for a moment, I thought I loved her. But then I remembered that there was a certain girl back home in the Midwest to whom I was still writing letters every week. And although I knew I shouldn't, I was signing those letters "Love, Nick." I knew I had to break it off with this girl before I was free.

Everyone has some goodness in them in one way or another. For myself, I believe my goodness comes from the fact that I am one of the few honest people that I have ever known.

Chapter 7

That summer, the most rich and powerful people in the country came to Gatsby's house. Even some people from far away—some as far as Europe—came to his house. It was a very, very long list of people.

One morning in late July, at around nine o'clock, Gatsby's beautiful car pulled up to my door and gave a burst of sound from its horn. It was the first time he had ever come to visit me, although I had gone to two of his parties, ridden on his boat, and often used his beach.

"Good morning, old sport. You're having

lunch with me today," said Gatsby. He saw me admiring his car.

"It's pretty, isn't it, old sport?" he said, and he jumped out of the car. "Haven't you ever seen it before?"

I had seen it. Everybody had seen it. It was a rich cream color, with light purple leather seats. I got into the car and off we drove to the city.

I had talked to Gatsby about six times in the past month, and I was disappointed to find out that he didn't really have much to say. So my first idea of him as a man of some importance quickly disappeared. Instead, I thought of him simply as a rich man with a big house next door.

But then we had this strange little ride into the city. We hadn't even left West Egg before Gatsby started acting strangely. He didn't finish his sentences and he started slapping his knee as if he were thinking hard about something.

"Look here, old sport," he finally said, "what's your opinion of me?"

I was a little surprised and couldn't answer right away. But Gatsby kept talking.

"I'm going to tell you something about my life," he said. "I don't want you to get the wrong idea of me. There are all these false stories of me floating around. I'll tell you the truth: I am the son of some wealthy people in the Midwest. They're all dead now. I was raised in America but educated at Oxford, because all my family have been educated there for many years. It's a family tradition."

He looked at me quickly, and I knew then why Jordan Baker didn't believe him. It was the way he rushed through some of the details, as if they bothered him. Now I didn't believe him either.

"What part of the Midwest?" I asked.

"San Francisco," he said.

"I see."

"My family died and left me all their

money." He looked serious. To me, at least this statement seemed true.

"For a while, I lived like a king, just traveling and spending money and living only for myself. I was trying to forget something very sad that had happened to me. But then came the war, old sport. I tried very hard to die, but for some reason I was never killed. Instead, I ended up leading a group of soldiers far into enemy territory and making the Germans in that area surrender. I was given awards from every government in the Allied forces. Even little Montenegro down in the Adriatic Sea!"

He reached into his pocket and pulled out a piece of metal attached to a bit of ribbon. He put it in my hand.

"That's the one from Montenegro," he said.

I was shocked. The thing looked real!

"Turn it," he said.

I did, and I read his name on the backside of the military award.

"Here's another thing I always carry. It

reminds me of my Oxford days." He gave me a photograph, where a bunch of young men were relaxing on the grass in front of a school that looked like Oxford. Gatsby, a little younger, was in the crowd.

So it was all true! This was evidence of his past.

"I'm going to make a big request of you today," he said, "so I wanted you to know something about me. You see, I surround myself with people I don't know so I can forget the sad thing that happened to me. But you'll hear about it this afternoon. I found out that you're taking Miss Baker to tea today. I asked her to tell you about it."

I had no idea what he was talking about, and I was a little upset with him. Why did he have to ruin my tea with Jordan? I didn't ask her to go to tea with me just to talk about Gatsby. But he wouldn't say another word, and we continued to drive to the city.

At noon, Gatsby and I walked into a

restaurant on Forty-second Street. Gatsby introduced me to a man who was waiting for us in the restaurant.

"Mr. Carraway, this is my friend Mr. Wolfsheim," Gatsby said.

A small, flat-nosed man raised his large head and looked at me with his tiny eyes. He shook my hand. Gatsby led us both to a table and we sat down.

"I like this place," Mr. Wolfsheim said, "but I like across the street better."

"It's too hot there," Gatsby said, looking at his menu.

"Hot and small, yes," said Mr. Wolfsheim, "but full of memories."

"What place is that?" I asked.

"The old Metropole," said Mr. Wolfsheim. "It's filled with faces dead and gone. Filled with friends now gone forever. I can't forget for as long as I live the night they shot Rosy Rosenthal there. There were six of us at the table, and Rosy drank a lot all evening. It was almost morning when the waiter came up with a strange look and said, 'There's somebody who wants to speak with you outside.' Rosy said 'All right,' and began to get up from his chair. But I pulled him back down and said, 'Let them come in here if they want you, but don't you move out of this room!'" Mr. Wolfsheim paused.

"Did he go?" I asked.

"Sure he went," Mr. Wolfsheim said. "He turned around at the door and said, 'Don't let that waiter take away my coffee!' Then he went out to the street, and they shot him three times in his stomach and drove away."

I remembered reading the news about it. Rosy Rosenthal was a gangster who was famous around New York. He was known for gambling and selling liquor. "Four men were sentenced to death in the trial," I said.

"Five," Mr. Wolfsheim said. Then he looked at me in an interested way. "So I understand you're looking for a business connection," he said.

Gatsby jumped in. "Oh, no," he said. "This isn't the man."

"No?" Mr. Wolfsheim looked disappointed.

"No, this is just a friend," said Gatsby. "I told you we would talk about that some other time."

"I beg your pardon, I thought you were another man," said Mr. Wolfsheim.

Our lunch arrived, and we began to eat.

"Look here, old sport," said Gatsby to me, "I'm afraid I made you rather angry in the car earlier."

"I don't know what this is all about, and I don't like mysteries," I said. "Why can't you just tell me what you want? Why does it have to come through Miss Baker?"

"Oh, don't worry, old sport. It's nothing bad," said Gatsby. Suddenly he looked at his watch, jumped up, and walked away from the table.

"He has to use the telephone," said Mr.

Wolfsheim. He had finished his lunch and was now drinking his coffee. "Gatsby's a fine fellow, isn't he? He's handsome and a perfect gentleman."

"Yes," I said.

"He's an Oxford man," said Mr. Wolfsheim. "It's one of the most famous colleges in the world."

"Have you known Gatsby for a long time?" I asked.

"Several years," he answered. "I met him right after the war." He paused and said, "I see you're looking at my shirt buttons."

I wasn't looking at them, but now that he directed my attention to them I did. They were made of strange white shapes. They looked like bone.

"The finest examples of human teeth," said Mr. Wolfsheim.

"Oh!" I said in shock.

Just then Gatsby returned and Wolfsheim got up to leave.

"Well, I should be going now," he said. "I have enjoyed my lunch, but I am much older than either of you, and I should be going." Mr. Wolfsheim shook our hands and walked away.

"He's quite a character," said Gatsby, watching his friend walk out of the restaurant.

"Who is he? An actor?"

"No, he's a gambler," said Gatsby. "He's the man who arranged for the Chicago White Sox to lose the World Series in 1919."

I was shocked. "That's the man who set up the World Series? That was a terrible scandal! How did he do that?"

"He just saw the opportunity," said Gatsby.

"Why isn't he in prison?"

"They can't get him, old sport. He's a very smart man."

Chapter 8

That afternoon, I had tea with Jordan Baker as planned. She sat very straight in her chair at the Plaza Hotel and began to tell her story.

"One October day in 1917," she said, "I was walking on the street outside of Daisy Fay's house. Daisy was eighteen years old at the time—two years older than me. She was the most popular girl in our town, Louisville. She dressed in white and had a little white car. All day long the telephone rang in her house and excited young army officers would ask to see her.

"I saw her that morning, sitting in her car

with a handsome young army officer. I had never seen him before. They were talking with such passion to each other that she didn't even see me until I was five feet away.

"'Hello, Jordan!' she called out to me. 'Please come here.'

"I was happy she was speaking to me because of all the older girls, I admired her most. She asked if I was going to the Red Cross that evening to make bandages. I told her I was. She asked if I would mind telling them that she couldn't come that day. The officer looked at Daisy while she was speaking in a way that every girl hopes to be looked at some time. His name was Jay Gatsby. I never saw him again until four years later. Even after I met him on Long Island, I didn't realize it was the same man.

"That was 1917. By the next year I had become more popular and I was playing in golf tournaments so I didn't see Daisy often. There were some wild stories around town about her. Some said her mother found her one night packing her bags and saying she was going to New York to say goodbye to some soldier who was going to war. Her mother stopped her, but Daisy didn't speak to her family for a long time after that.

"By the next autumn she was lively again—as lively as ever. In February she seemed to be engaged to a man from New Orleans, but in June she married Tom Buchanan of Chicago. It was the biggest wedding Louisville had ever seen. He came down with a hundred people in four private cars. The day before the wedding he gave her a string of pearls that was worth three hundred thousand dollars.

"I was invited to her wedding. I went into her room half an hour before the wedding dinner and found Daisy lying on her bed, completely drunk. She had a bottle in one hand and a letter in the other.

"'What's the matter?' I asked.

"'Here, dearest,' she said and handed me

a waste basket. In it was the string of pearls. 'Go and tell them Daisy changed her mind!' She began to cry and cry. I ran downstairs and got another woman to help. Together, we locked the door and put Daisy in a cold bath. She wouldn't let go of her letter. She only agreed to put it on the soap dish when we showed her that it was falling apart in the water.

"But she didn't say anything else. The next day, she married Tom Buchanan, and they left for a three-month trip to the South Seas.

"I saw them in Santa Barbara when they returned from their trip. Daisy seemed to be completely in love with Tom. She would sit with his head in her lap and run her fingers through his hair for hours. A week after I left Santa Barbara, I heard Tom got into a car accident. There was a woman in the car, too. She also got into the newspapers because her arm was broken. She was a maid at a hotel in Santa Barbara.

"The next April, they went to France for a year. Then they lived in Chicago. Daisy was very popular in Chicago. But they decided to move to Long Island, and now here they are.

"About six weeks ago, Daisy heard the name Gatsby for the first time in years. It was when I asked you—do you remember?—if you knew Gatsby in West Egg. After you left that night, Daisy came to my room and asked, 'Who is Gatsby?' When I described him, she said in the strangest voice that it must be the man she used to know. Then I realized he must have been the young officer in her white car."

By the time Jordan finished telling me all of this, we had left the Plaza Hotel and were driving through Central Park.

"Gatsby bought that house so Daisy would be just across the bay," said Jordan.

I remembered the first night I saw Gatsby. He had stood at the edge of his lawn and stretched his arms out across the bay.

"He wants to know if you'll invite Daisy to your house some afternoon and then let him come over," she said.

I couldn't believe it. The man had waited five years just so he could "come over" some afternoon in the hopes of running into Daisy.

"Did I have to know all this before he could ask me such a little thing?" I asked.

"He's afraid," said Jordan. "He's waited so long. He thought you might not like it."

"Why didn't he ask you to arrange a meeting?"

"He wants her to see his house," she explained. "And your house is right next door."

"Oh!"

"I think he sort of expected her to wander into one of his parties some night," said Jordan. "But she never did. Then he began asking people if they knew her, and I was the first one he found. It was that night that he called me into his library to speak to me. But when I said you were a friend of Tom's, he seemed to not want to go through with it at all."

It was getting dark, and the ride through Central Park felt nice. Suddenly I wasn't thinking of Gatsby or Daisy but only of Jordan, sitting next to me.

"Daisy ought to have something nice in her life," said Jordan.

"Does she want to see Gatsby?"

"She's not supposed to know about it. He doesn't want her to know. You're just supposed to invite her to tea."

We passed a block of apartments, and they threw soft yellow light from the windows. I drew Jordan closer to me. She smiled her proud little smile, so I kissed her.

Chapter 9

That night when I came home, I saw Gatsby on his lawn. He saw me and walked over.

"Hello, old sport," he said. "Let's go to Coney Island. We'll go in my car."

"It's too late," I said.

"Well, how about going for a swim in my pool then?"

He sounded very eager to please me.

"I've got to go to bed," I said.

"All right." He stood there looking at me, as if he didn't want me to go in yet. I knew why he was hanging around—he wanted to know whether I was going to invite Daisy to tea.

"I talked with Miss Baker," I said. "I'm going to call Daisy tomorrow and invite her to come over to tea."

"Oh, that's all right," he said, trying to sound like he didn't care. "I don't want to trouble you."

"What day would be best for you?" I asked.

"What day would be best for *you*?" he replied. "I really don't want to trouble you."

So we agreed on the day after tomorrow. But he insisted on paying somebody to cut my grass before she came. The next day, I called Daisy and invited her to tea. I told her not to bring Tom.

It was pouring rain on the day of the tea. In the morning, a man came to cut my grass in the heavy rain. Then Gatsby sent over many bunches of flowers, which his servants arranged all over my house. Then, about an hour later, Gatsby himself showed up at my door. He was wearing a white suit, a silver shirt, and a gold tie. He looked very pale and tired, as if he didn't get any sleep the night before.

He sat on a chair in my living room and looked very anxious for about half an hour. Then he suddenly got up and said he was going home.

"What?" I asked. "Why?"

"Nobody is coming to tea. It's too late!"

"Calm down," I said. "It's two minutes to four o'clock. She'll be here soon."

Just then, we heard a car coming up the road. We both jumped up. I went out into the yard. Daisy's car came slowly up to the house, and I saw her face smiling at me from the window.

"Is this where you live, my dearest one?" she asked me in her beautiful, musical voice.

"Yes, Daisy, do come in," I said. I took her hand and helped her out of the car. We went in. I was shocked to find the living room was empty. Gatsby was nowhere in sight.

"Well, that's funny!" I said.

"What's funny?" Daisy asked, looking around her. Then there was a light knock at the door. I went out and opened it. There stood Gatsby, as pale as death, standing with his hands stuck deep in his coat pockets. He was completely wet and he stared helplessly into my eyes. He must have gone out the back door and walked around the house.

Without saying anything, Gatsby walked past me and turned into the living room. My heart was beating hard as I listened to the silence that followed.

Then I heard a strange, almost painful laugh come from Daisy, and I heard her say, "Well, I'm certainly glad to see you again."

More silence followed. I couldn't stand it, so I joined them in the living room. Daisy sat stiff, straight, and scared on a chair. Gatsby leaned against the wall by a little shelf. He was trying to look natural and was doing a terrible job. As he leaned back, his head knocked over a clock on the little shelf, and he turned quickly and caught it.

"I'm sorry," he said to me.

Everybody was so uncomfortable that we didn't know what to do. Finally the maid came in from the kitchen carrying a tray with our tea. With the business of handing out cups and plates and pouring tea, we became a little more comfortable with each other. I took the first moment I could to excuse myself to leave Gatsby and Daisy alone.

"Where are you going?" asked Gatsby, looking very worried.

"I'll be back in a bit," I said. Then as I walked out the door, Gatsby followed me.

"Wait, I have to talk to you about something," he said. He and I hurried into the kitchen. Once the door closed behind us, Gatsby put his head in his hands.

"This was a mistake," he said, "a terrible, terrible mistake."

"Don't worry, you're just embarrassed," I

said. "Daisy is embarrassed too."

"She is?" asked Gatsby. He didn't sound like he believed me.

"Yes, just as much as you are," I said. "You're acting like a little boy. Plus, you're being rude. Daisy is sitting in there all alone."

At that, Gatsby straightened up. He gave me a long look and walked back into the living room. I walked in the other direction, out the back door and into the yard. The rain was lighter now, and I was able to spend about half an hour comfortably under a big tree. After I felt that enough time had passed, I went back inside.

In the living room, I found a completely different scene from the one I had left. Daisy and Gatsby sat together, staring into each other's eyes. All their discomfort was gone. Daisy's face was covered with tears, and she began wiping them away as I walked in. Gatsby seemed to glow with happiness.

"Hello, old sport," he said. He smiled his

big, beautiful smile at me.

"It stopped raining," I said.

"Has it?" He looked out the window and said to Daisy, "Well look at that! It stopped raining."

Daisy looked at him with big, happy eyes and smiled. "I'm so glad, Jay," she said.

"I want you and Daisy to come over to my house," said Gatsby. "I'd like to show her around."

Daisy went upstairs to wash her face, and Gatsby and I waited for her outside.

"My house looks nice, doesn't it?" Gatsby asked. "Look how it catches the light."

I agreed that it was very beautiful.

"It took me just three years to earn the money that bought it."

I realized I still didn't know what Gatsby did for work. When I asked, Gatsby said, "Oh, this and that. I was in the medicine business, then the oil business. But I'm not in either now."

It was a strange and unclear answer. I still had the uneasy feeling that he made his money in some way that was against the law.

Then Daisy came out. "Your house is that huge place *there*?" she said in shock.

We walked to the house, taking our time through his big yard and crossing his beach. When we entered the house, it was strangely quiet. I expected party guests to pop up at every corner, but nobody was there. We walked through bedrooms, guest rooms, music rooms, and the library. It was all so grand that Daisy kept making little noises of surprise, saying how much she admired the house.

Gatsby never took his eyes off of Daisy. In fact, it seemed like he judged the worth of his many things by Daisy's responses to them. Sometimes, too, he looked around at his house in a surprised way, as though he couldn't believe all of it was his.

Gatsby's bedroom was the simplest room of

all. Daisy walked about it in wonder. Gatsby opened his closet and showed us all his beautiful clothes inside. There were suits and ties and robes and piles of shirts folded neatly.

"I've got a man in England who buys my clothes. He sends a selection of things at the beginning of each season."

He laughed and took out a pile of shirts and began throwing them, one by one, before us. While we admired, he brought out more and more, and the soft, rich pile grew higher. Suddenly, Daisy bent her head into the shirts and began to cry.

"They're such beautiful shirts!" she said. "I've never seen such—such beautiful shirts before!" Her tears rolled down her face, and she smiled, so bright and so sad.

After that, we walked to the window and looked across the bay. It was raining lightly again.

"If it wasn't raining we could see your home across the bay," said Gatsby. "You always have a green light that burns all night at the end of your dock."

Daisy put her arm through his, but he didn't seem to notice. He was staring across the water. Perhaps he had just realized that the importance of that light had disappeared forever. Compared to the great distance that had separated them, that green light had always seemed very near to her—almost touching her. It had seemed as close as a star to the moon. Now that he had finally reached Daisy, it became just another light.

I looked around the room and saw a photograph that interested me. It was of an old man dressed in boat clothes.

"Who is this?" I asked.

"That's Mr. Dan Cody, old sport. He's dead now. He used to be my best friend years ago."

"Come here, quick!" said Daisy, who was still at the window. We went over and looked. The rain had just stopped and the sun was setting, streaming bright light through pink and gold clouds.

"Look at that, Jay," Daisy whispered. "I'd like to get one of those pink clouds and put you in it and push you around."

As Daisy and Gatsby stood there, I decided to go home. I started to say goodbye but stopped myself. I noticed something in Gatsby's face. He looked ever so slightly troubled, as if he were puzzled about something. I realized then that Daisy, no matter how lovely she was, could never be as perfect as Gatsby had made her in his mind. It was not her fault. Too much time had passed—Gatsby had waited five long years! In every memory of her, he had made her greater and lovelier than any human ever could be. Now, perhaps he was beginning to realize the difference between his imagined Daisy and his real one. I watched him as he took her hand. Then Daisy said something into his ear and he looked at her with a rush of emotion. Her voice, beautiful and musical, was one thing that could not be over-dreamed. Her voice was better than any imagined song.

They continued to look out the window. They had forgotten me. I looked once more at them and quietly walked home, leaving them there together.

Chapter 10

Gatsby told me much later that his name was actually James Gatz. He was from North Dakota, and his parents were poor farming people. They led a life that he didn't want, and in his own mind, he never quite accepted that they were his parents at all.

When James Gatz was sixteen years old, he left home to find a new life for himself. He already had a new name picked out—Jay Gatsby. The first person he told it to was Dan Cody.

For about a year, Gatsby had been working around Lake Superior, fishing and helping people with their boats. But every day, he imagined a beautiful future for himself. He imagined huge houses, wealth, and riches. Every day, he added another beautiful detail to his dream.

One day, as he was walking along the beach looking for something to do, he came across Dan Cody's large yacht. Cody was stopped there for the night, but Gatsby knew a dangerous storm was coming. Cody was fifty years old then, and very, very rich. Gatsby saw an opportunity. He borrowed a rowboat and rowed over to Cody's yacht. He introduced himself as Jay Gatsby and told Cody he better move to a safer place because of the storm that was quickly approaching.

Cody was traveling alone. His wife had married him for his money and was not a very nice woman. So for five years, he had been moving from place to place in his yacht trying to seek some happiness. And suddenly, here was this young man who was smart, independent, and eager to help. Cody liked Gatsby instantly. After asking Gatsby a few questions, Cody decided to hire him. A few days later, Cody took Gatsby into town and bought him a blue coat, six pairs of white pants, and a hat. When the yacht left for the West Indies, Gatsby went too.

Gatsby was hired to do many things for Cody, including some rather personal work. Cody liked to drink, and he knew he made bad decisions when he drank too much. So, one of Gatsby's jobs was to make sure Cody stayed in his room when he drank. The two men enjoyed having each other around, and Gatsby worked for Cody for five years. During that time, they traveled all over the world. But it all ended when Cody's wife came onto the yacht in Boston one day, and Cody died a week later.

Cody had left Gatsby twenty-five thousand dollars, but Gatsby never got it. Cody's wife somehow managed to get all of Cody's money, which totaled several million dollars.

Chapter 11

One day later that summer, Gatsby finally met Tom. It happened by accident—Tom was riding horses with two of his friends, and they rode onto Gatsby's land without knowing it. I was there, visiting Gatsby. He invited them inside and we all sat down for a drink.

"I'm delighted to see you," said Gatsby, shaking Tom's hand. "We're neighbors. Please, sit down. What can I get you to drink?"

Gatsby watched Tom closely. Tom, of course, had no idea who Gatsby was. At some point while we all talked, Gatsby said to Tom, "I know your wife." I paused and stared. It seemed like Gatsby was testing Tom somehow.

"Oh, do you?" asked Tom. Then he turned to me. "You live near here, Nick?"

"Next door," I said.

Tom and his friends left shortly afterward. But that Saturday, Tom and Daisy finally came to one of Gatsby's parties. They arrived just as it was getting dark, and Gatsby and I met them out in the yard. We walked among crowds of people toward the house.

"This is so exciting!" Daisy said.

"Look around," said Gatsby, "you must recognize some of the people here. There are many famous people here tonight. Singers, actors, politicians..."

"Well, we don't know many famous people," Tom said.

"What about her?" asked Gatsby, pointing to a very beautiful woman sitting under a tree. Tom and Daisy stared in shock. She was a famous movie star, perhaps one of the most famous at the time.

We wandered around, eating and drinking. Tom began talking with a group of people, and Daisy and Gatsby danced. I watched them and was surprised at what a good dancer Gatsby was. Then the two walked over to my house and sat on the steps for half an hour. I stayed in the garden and watched for anybody who might come that way.

As we were sitting down to dinner, Tom appeared again.

"Do you mind if I eat with those people over there?" he asked. "There's a man who's saying some interesting things..."

"Go ahead," said Daisy. Then she watched as Tom went to sit with a girl, not a man as he had said.

"She's rather pretty," Daisy said. I knew then that aside from the time she had spent with Gatsby, she was not having a good time. We were sitting at a table with very drunk people. That was my fault, because I knew them and had had a good time with them here a few weeks before. But what seemed fun a few weeks ago now seemed to be in bad taste. A girl was very drunk and was trying to lean her head on my shoulder. An older woman was talking very loudly about how the girl always drank too much. Daisy, who didn't drink at all, seemed very uncomfortable.

The evening went on in this way. When Daisy and Tom decided to leave, I waited with them for their car.

"What does this Gatsby do for work, anyway?" asked Tom. "What is he, some big gangster?"

"No, he owned a bunch of stores that sold medicine," said Daisy. "The stores made him very rich."

"Most of these newly rich people are just big gangsters," Tom said. "And he must have worked hard to get this crazy scene together. Daisy didn't like it," he said to me. "Did you see her face when that drunk girl almost fell over her?"

Daisy didn't respond and started to sing. Her strange, beautiful voice carried on the wind until their car arrived and they left.

I stayed at Gatsby's house. He had asked me to wait for him until he was free. Finally, when the last guest had gone upstairs and the last bedroom light turned off, Gatsby came to find me.

"She didn't like it," he said immediately.

"Of course she did."

"No, she didn't. She didn't have a good time," he insisted. "I feel far away from her. It's hard to make her understand."

I knew what Gatsby wanted. He wanted Daisy to tell Tom, "I never loved you." After she destroyed their four years of marriage like this, Gatsby wanted to take her back to Louisville where they would get married. It would be like their five years apart never happened.

"She doesn't understand," he said. "She

used to be able to understand. We would sit for hours—"

He broke off and started walking down a dark path covered in crushed flowers and broken glass.

"Don't ask too much of her," I said. "You can't repeat the past."

"Can't repeat the past?" he cried in shock. "Why of course you can!" He looked around wildly, as if he was looking for the past hiding right there in his garden.

Chapter 12

All of a sudden, there were no more parties at Gatsby's house. Every weekend throughout the summer, there had been bright lights and laughter and music at his house. Now there was nothing but silence.

I went over there one afternoon to see if he was all right. A mean-looking man answered his door.

"Is Mr. Gatsby sick?" I asked.

"No," said the man.

"I haven't seen him lately, and I was a little worried. Please tell him Mr. Carraway came over," I said.

The man agreed and shut the door in my face. I found out later that Gatsby had let every servant in his house go. He had replaced them with about six new people that no one had ever seen before. They did not go into to town to order food or drink. People in town said that the people were not servants at all.

The next day, Gatsby called me on the phone.

"Are you going away?" I asked. "I heard you fired all your servants."

"I wanted people who wouldn't talk about my private matters to others," he said, "because Daisy comes over quite often in the afternoons now. So I hired some people that Wolfsheim knows."

"I see," I said.

Then he told me that Daisy wanted me to come to her house for lunch the next day. Miss Baker would be there too, he said.

The next day was hot—it was one of the last days of summer, and it was definitely the hottest day of the year. Gatsby and I went together to Daisy's house. When we entered the living room, Daisy and Jordan were both dressed in white and laying on the couch.

"It's too hot to move!" they both said.

Tom entered the room. He saw us and greeted Gatsby first. He hid his dislike for him well.

"Mr. Gatsby!" he said, holding out his hand. "I'm glad to see you, sir."

"Make us a cold drink!" cried Daisy.

As Tom left the room again, Daisy got up and went over to Gatsby. She pulled his face down and kissed him on the mouth.

"You know I love you," she said to him.

"You forget there are other people in the room," said Jordan, lightly laughing.

"I don't care!" said Daisy, smiling. But she sat back down next to Jordan on the couch. Just then Tom entered again with four full glasses. We all took one and drank them quickly, the ice knocking against the glass. We had lunch outside in the shade. There was an anxious kind of feeling all throughout lunch, and it made me uncomfortable.

"What will we do with ourselves this afternoon?" asked Daisy when we had finished. Jordan and I looked at her. Tom was having a conversation with Gatsby.

"I know! Let's go into town!" cried Daisy.

Tom just kept talking to Gatsby, not paying any attention to her.

"Who wants to go into town?" Daisy demanded. Gatsby's eyes floated toward her. "Ah," she cried, "you look so cool."

Their eyes met, and they stared at each other, as if they were alone. Daisy finally forced herself to look down at the table.

"You always look so cool," she repeated.

In that little moment, Daisy had silently told Gatsby that she loved him, and Tom Buchanan saw it. He was shocked. His mouth opened a little, and he just looked at Gatsby, and then back at Daisy.

"All right," Tom said. "Let's go to town. Come on, we're all going to town."

He stood up suddenly, his eyes still flashing between Daisy and Gatsby. No one moved.

"Come on!" he said angrily. "What's the matter? If we're going to town, let's go now!"

Tom's hand, shaking a little, brought his glass to his lips and he took another drink. We all moved out to where the cars were parked.

"Shall we all go in my car?" Gatsby asked.

"No," said Tom. "You take my car and I'll take yours. Come on, Daisy. I'll drive you in this crazy yellow thing."

"No, you take Jordan and Nick," Daisy said. "I'll go with Gatsby." She walked close to Gatsby. As they got into Tom's little blue car, Jordan, Tom, and I got into Gatsby's. Tom started the car and sped off, leaving Daisy and Gatsby in the dust.

"Did you see that?" he demanded, as we got on the road.

"See what?"

He looked at Jordan and me with narrowed eyes. He realized that we must have known about Daisy and Gatsby all along.

"You must think I'm blind, don't you?" he said. "Well I know some things when I see it, and I never liked that man! And I've found out some things about him. I would have found out more if I had known..."

"Tom, if you didn't like him why did you invite him to lunch?" Jordan demanded.

"I didn't! Daisy did! She knew him before we were married—I hate to think how they ever met."

We drove along unhappily in the heat. When the eyes of Doctor T. J. Eckleburg came into sight, I reminded Tom that we needed gas. He pulled off the road angrily and stopped at Wilson's garage. After a while, Wilson appeared at the door and stared at the car.

"We want some gas!" Tom cried out.

"What do you think we stopped for? To admire the view?"

"I'm sick," said Wilson. He didn't move. His face looked green and he truly looked ill.

"Well, do I need to help myself?" Tom shouted. With an effort, Wilson walked over to the car and helped us with the gas.

"How do you like this car?" Tom asked Wilson.

"It's a nice yellow one," Wilson said, working with the gas.

"I'll sell you this one instead of my blue car," said Tom. "How about it?"

"I can't afford this," said Wilson, "but I would like to buy your other car. I need it soon. I'm taking my wife away from here."

Now Tom looked shocked.

"Taking her away? Where? And why?"

Wilson finished with the gas. "She's been telling me for the past ten years that she wants to go out West. Now I'm taking her there whether she wants to go or not."

"Why?" asked Tom again.

"Because I just found out that she's been fooling around with some other man around here."

Tom stared for a moment. Then he asked, "How much do I owe you for the gas?"

"A dollar and twenty cents."

Just then, I got the feeling that we were being watched. I looked up at Wilson's garage and noticed that Myrtle was watching us from a window. I watched as the look on her face changed from shock to anger to something else—was it jealousy? Then I realized her eyes were not fixed on Tom, but on Jordan Baker, whom she assumed was his wife.

Daisy and Gatsby caught up to us on the road and we all ended up at the Plaza Hotel. We were all so tired and unhappy from the heat that hardly any of us knew what we were doing. We rented a hotel room with the idea that it would be cool. But sooner or later, we found ourselves in a room that was just as hot as being outside. We looked around unhappily at each other. Daisy went to the mirror and began fixing her hair.

"Open a window," she demanded.

"It's already open," said Jordan.

"Open another one."

"There aren't any more."

"We should forget the heat," cut in Tom. "You make it ten times worse, Daisy, by complaining about it all the time."

"Why don't you leave her alone, old sport?" said Gatsby. "You're the one who insisted we come to town."

There was a moment of silence.

"That's a great expression of yours, isn't it?" asked Tom with a mean smile on his face. "All this 'old sport' business. Where did you pick that up?"

"Now look here, Tom. If you're going to make personal remarks I'm not going to stay another minute," said Daisy. "Just call downstairs for some glasses and whiskey."

But Tom continued.

"I hear you're an Oxford man," he said, his eyes narrowing at Gatsby.

"I can't really say that, but I went there," said Gatsby.

"Oh, come on. Just admit to everybody you never went to Oxford. We all know it's a lie," said Tom.

"I did go there," said Gatsby. "It was 1919. I only stayed five months. That's why I can't really call myself an Oxford man."

Tom looked at all of us to see if we believed him. But we were all looking at Gatsby.

"It was an opportunity they gave to some of the officers after the war," Gatsby continued. "We could go to any of the universities in England or France."

So that was it! I was happy to find out that it was never a lie, that he had really gone to Oxford. But Tom was not finished.

"Well I have one more question for you,

Mr. Gatsby. What kind of trouble are you trying to start in my house, anyway?"

We all held our breath. The secret was out in the open now.

"He isn't causing trouble," broke in Daisy. "You're causing trouble. Please have a little self-control."

"Self-control?" Tom exploded. "I suppose I should sit back and let Mr. Nobody from Nowhere make love to my wife. Well, that's never going to happen. I know I'm not very popular. I don't throw big parties. But I suppose you have to turn your house into a circus every Saturday to have any friends!"

"I've got something to tell *you*, old sport—" began Gatsby. But Daisy cut in.

"Please don't!" she cried. "Let's all go home. Why don't we all go home?"

"That's a good idea," I said. "Come on, Tom. Nobody wants to stay here. Let's go."

"I want to know what Mr. Gatsby has to tell me."

"Your wife doesn't love you," said Gatsby. "She never loved you. She loves me."

"You must be crazy!" Tom shouted.

Gatsby jumped to his feet, shaking with excitement.

"She never loved you! She only married you because I was poor and she was tired of waiting for me. It was a terrible mistake but in her heart she never loved anyone but me!"

At this point Jordan and I tried to go, but Tom and Gatsby both insisted that we stay.

"That's a damn lie," said Tom. "Daisy loved me when she married me and she still does. And what's more, I love her too. Sometimes I make mistakes but I always come back, and in my heart I love her all the time."

"You're awful," said Daisy. She turned to me and said, "Do you know why we left Chicago? I'm surprised nobody has told you about *that* little mistake Tom made!"

Gatsby walked over and stood beside her. "Daisy, that's all over now," he said. "It doesn't matter any more. Just tell him the truth—that you never loved him—and it will be done forever."

Daisy paused. Her eyes fell on Jordan and me as if she was asking us what she should do. It was as if she finally realized what she was doing, but she had never intended to do anything at all. But it was done now. It was too late.

"I never loved him," she said. But it didn't sound true.

"Not in France?" asked Tom suddenly.

"No."

"Not that day I carried you down from the Plaza to keep your shoes dry?" Tom's voice shook.... "Daisy?"

"Please don't," she said. Then she looked at Gatsby. "There, Jay, I said it!"

She tried to light a cigarette but her hand was shaking. Then she threw the cigarette on the floor and shouted at Gatsby, "You want too much! I love you now, isn't that enough? I can't help what has passed." She began to cry. "I did love him once. But I loved you too."

"You loved me *too*?" Gatsby repeated. His eyes were wide with shock.

"That's a lie!" shouted Tom. "She didn't even know you were alive. There are things between Daisy and me that you'll never know, things that neither of us can ever forget."

Tom's words seemed to bite physically into Gatsby.

"I can't say I never loved Tom," cried Daisy. "It wouldn't be true!"

"Of course it wouldn't," agreed Tom.

"As if it mattered to you!" she shouted at her husband.

"You don't understand," said Gatsby to Tom, "she's leaving you."

"She's not leaving me! Not for some dirty gangster like you! You'd have to steal the ring to put on her finger! Who are you, anyway? You're one of that group that hangs around Meyer Wolfsheim. I know that about you. But

I'm going to find out more."

"That's fine," said Gatsby calmly.

"I found out what your 'medicine' stores were, too!" Tom turned to us and spoke rapidly. "He and this Wolfsheim character bought a lot of stores in poor neighborhoods. Then they sold illegal grain liquor there. And that's only one of his little tricks. I knew he was a criminal the first time I saw him!"

"So what?" said Gatsby. "One of your own friends, Walter Chase, did it too! But it's all right if one of your friends breaks the law, isn't it old sport?"

"Don't you call me 'old sport'!" cried Tom. "That 'medicine store' business was just small money for you. But now you've got some big deal going on with Wolfsheim that even Walter is too afraid to tell me about!"

Daisy's eyes looked to Tom and then to Gatsby in terror. Gatsby began to talk quickly to Daisy, telling her everything Tom said was untrue. But with every word, she was drawing further and further away from him.

"Oh, please, Tom!" she cried. "I can't stand this any more. Let's go home!"

"You and Mr. Gatsby go home in his car," said Tom. Daisy looked at him with fear in her eyes.

"It's all right, Daisy," Tom said in a slightly mean voice. "Mr. Gatsby won't bother you. I think he realizes all his tricks are over now."

Without a word, they left. All of a sudden, I realized something.

"I...I just remembered today is my birthday," I said.

I was thirty now. And stretching ahead of me was the dark, lonely road of a new decade.

At seven o'clock, Jordan, Tom, and I got into Tom's car and started driving home toward Long Island. All the way, Tom talked loudly and excitedly, knowing he had won.

Chapter 13

A young Greek man named Michaelis was the main witness of the accident. He lived across the street from Wilson's garage. At around five o'clock that evening, he went over to Wilson's and found him very sick in the office. Michaelis told him to go to bed, but Wilson refused. Then Michaelis heard yelling and a lot of noise coming from upstairs.

"I've got my wife locked in a room up there," Wilson said. "She's going to stay there until the day after tomorrow. Then I'm taking her away to the West."

Michaelis was shocked. He never thought

Wilson was the type of man who could do such things. Michaelis asked why, but Wilson didn't explain. Instead, he looked at Michaelis with narrowed eyes and began asking where he was and what he was doing on certain days in the recent past. Michaelis began to feel uneasy and went home. But at around seven o'clock that evening, he heard Mrs. Wilson's voice shouting from across the street.

"Beat me, then!" she was yelling at Wilson. "Throw me down and beat me, or are you too afraid to?"

A moment later, she rushed out into the darkening night. She was waving her hands and shouting. But before Michaelis could do anything, it was all over.

The "death car," as the newspapers called it, didn't stop. It came out of the darkness then disappeared around the next bend in the road. Michaelis wasn't even sure of the car's color. At first he told the police that it was light green. The other car, the one heading toward New York, stopped a few feet down the road. The driver got out and ran back to where Myrtle Wilson lay bleeding in the middle of the road. Michaelis ran to her too. When they reached her, they knew she was already dead.

As Tom, Jordan, and I drove home, we saw a crowd and three or four cars gathered on the side of the road. Tom slowed down and didn't seem like he was going to stop until he realized that the crowd was in front of Wilson's garage. Then he looked worried and stopped the car.

"We'll just take a quick look," he said.

As we walked toward the garage, we heard someone repeating over and over, "Oh, my God! Oh, my God! Oh, my God!" There was a crowd gathered around something. Tom stretched to look over people's heads and suddenly made a strange noise in his throat. Then he pushed people out of his way and moved toward the center of the crowd.

Myrtle Wilson's body lay on a table. She was wrapped in two blankets. Tom went to her side and just stood there, staring. I realized the person yelling "Oh, my God!" was Wilson. He stood to the side of the garage, in the doorway to his office. He rocked back and forth, staring at his wife's body, weeping and repeating those three words. A man was at his side, trying to speak softly to him.

Tom turned to a policeman taking notes. "Hey," he said roughly, "what happened here? I need to know!"

"A car hit her. She was instantly killed."

"Instantly killed?" repeated Tom, staring.

"She ran out in the road. The driver didn't even stop his car."

"There were two cars," said Michaelis, "going opposite ways. One was coming from New York and the other was going. She ran out there and the one coming from New York knocked right into her, going thirty or forty miles an hour."

Another man stepped forward. "It was a big yellow car," he said.

"Did you see the accident?" asked the policeman.

"No, but the car passed me down the road, going much faster than forty miles an hour. Maybe fifty or sixty."

Suddenly, Wilson yelled out to the crowd. He had heard part of this conversation.

"You don't have to tell me what kind of car it was! I know it! I saw it today!" he cried out. Tom got very stiff, and after a moment, he walked over to Wilson. He took the thin man by his shoulders and began talking to him in a low voice.

"Listen, I just got here a minute ago from New York," he said. "I was bringing you my car that you wanted to buy from me. That yellow car I was driving this afternoon wasn't mine. Do you understand me? I haven't seen it all afternoon."

Wilson just stared at him. Tom picked up

Wilson as lightly as if he were a doll, and carried him into the office. He sat him down in a chair and came back out.

"Somebody ought to sit with him and watch him," he said to the crowd. Then he turned to me and said, "Let's go."

After Jordan, Tom, and I were back in the car, Tom drove slowly at first, then drove faster and faster. He began to cry. "He didn't even stop his car!" he said.

When we reached Tom's house, we saw there were several lights on.

"Daisy's home," he said, and we all got out of the car. As we walked toward the house, Tom invited us to have some supper and offered to call me a taxi to take me home.

"I don't want any food right now," I said. "I'll just stay out here and wait for the taxi."

I was feeling a little sick and I wanted to be alone. I didn't even want to be with Jordan.

"It's only nine-thirty," said Jordan. But I had had enough of all of them, and something in my face must have told her so. She looked hurt, and then quickly turned and walked into the house. When they had all gone, I sat down on the steps with my head in my hands. Then I heard footsteps coming toward me. When I looked up, I saw Gatsby, half hidden in the darkness.

"What are you doing?" I asked.

"Just standing here, old sport."

I was sick of him too. I wanted to go home.

"Did you see any trouble on the road?" he asked after a minute.

"Yes."

He paused.

"Was she killed?"

"Yes."

"I thought so. I told Daisy I thought so. But she didn't want to stop. I think she was too shocked. I got us back to West Egg on a smaller side road and hid the car in my garage," he said. "Who was the woman?"

"Her name was Myrtle Wilson. Her

husband owns the garage there. How the hell did it happen?" I demanded. I disliked him so much now.

"Well, I tried to swing the wheel..." He didn't finish, and suddenly I guessed at the truth.

"Was Daisy driving?"

"Yes," he said. "But of course I'll say I was driving if anybody asks. You see, when we left New York she was feeling very bad and she thought it would calm her if she drove. And this woman just rushed into the road out of nowhere...We were about to pass another car coming the other way. It all happened in a moment, but it seemed like she was coming toward us to speak to us. First, Daisy turned away from the woman toward the other car, but then she was afraid of hitting the car and turned back. The second my hand reached the wheel, we had hit her...It must have killed her instantly."

"It ripped her open—"

"Don't tell me, old sport." His face looked pained. "Well, Daisy just sped up. I tried to make her stop, but she just couldn't. I finally made her, and she just fell over into my lap. Then I drove us to my house. I think she'll be all right tomorrow," he said, looking up at the windows. "I'm just going to wait here and see if Tom tries to bother her. She locked herself in her room. If he tries to hurt her, she's going to turn the light off and then on again, so I'll know."

"He won't touch her," I said.

"I don't trust him, old sport."

"How long are you going to wait?"

"All night, if necessary."

"You wait here," I said. "I'll take a look around."

I walked back toward the kitchen softly, and looked up into the window. I saw Daisy and Tom sitting at the kitchen table, facing each other. There was a plate of cold chicken between them, and two bottles of beer. He was talking to her, and sometimes she would look up at him and nod.

They weren't happy, but they weren't unhappy either. There was definitely the feeling of a man and his wife planning something together.

I walked quietly back toward Gatsby. He was waiting for me.

"Is it all quiet up there?" he asked anxiously.

"Yes, it's all quiet." I added, "You better come home and get some sleep."

He shook his head.

"I want to wait here until Daisy goes to bed. Good night, old sport."

Then he turned back to the house eagerly, as if he didn't want me to bother him as he watched the house. So I walked away and left him standing there—watching over nothing.

Chapter 14

I couldn't sleep all night. I had terrible dreams and kept waking up. Sometime toward dawn, I heard a taxi go up Gatsby's road, and I knew he was returning from Daisy's house. I got up, got dressed, and walked over.

Gatsby saw me coming across his yard. He looked tired.

"Nothing happened," he said. "I waited, and at about four o'clock she came to the window and stood there for a minute and then turned out the light."

His house was huge, but it never seemed bigger than that morning. We walked from room to room, looking for cigarettes. When we finally found some, we went outside and smoked silently.

"You ought to go away," I finally said.

"Go away *now*, old sport?" He wouldn't hear of it. He couldn't possibly leave Daisy now. He was holding onto some last hope and I couldn't bear to shake him free.

It was this morning that he told me about Dan Cody and his past. He also told me how he met Daisy. He was a young officer in the army, about to be sent to Europe for the war. Before he went, he was stationed at Camp Taylor, in Louisville, for a month. He went over to Daisy's house one day with a group of other invited officers. Her house was the most beautiful house he had ever seen, and he remembered walking through it in wonder.

When he met Daisy, the first thing he noticed was her voice. He heard so much *money* in it. It was a rich voice—the voice of a lovely girl who had grown up in a lovely house, whose whole life had been lovely. It was a mystery to him, and he wanted to know more.

Gatsby was surprised when he fell in love with Daisy. And he was surprised when she fell in love with him too. He knew things that she didn't know because of all his travels and experiences. He had such great dreams and plans for his future. But telling Daisy about all the things he planned to do was suddenly more fun than actually doing them. Right then and there, he decided to give his plans, his dreams, and his life to Daisy.

On the night before he went to Europe, he sat with Daisy in his arms for a long time. They didn't say much, but they touched each other's hands, and once he kissed her dark shining hair. They told each other without words how much they loved each other.

He did very well in the war, but all he wanted to do after the war was to go back home. However, the army made a mistake and sent him to Oxford instead. He started to get worried. Daisy's letters to him were starting to sound as if she were giving up on waiting. She couldn't understand why he couldn't come home. Meanwhile, life went on for Daisy. As much as she missed Gatsby, there were still parties for her to go to, young men to dance with, friends who still expected to see her every evening. She simply couldn't stop the passing of time.

Then, in the middle of spring, Tom Buchanan came along. There was something so solid and reassuring about him. Gatsby could only offer her promises, while Tom offered her reality. After the wedding, Daisy wrote to Gatsby. Her letter reached him while he was still at Oxford.

When Gatsby returned from Oxford, he made one last visit to Louisville just to walk down the same streets he and Daisy used to walk down together. Then he went to New York to make his fortune.

It was around nine o'clock in the morning

when Gatsby finished telling me this. We had breakfast, then we went outside. The weather was now mild—it would be another warm, late summer day. The gardener told Gatsby he would empty the pool that day.

"The leaves will start falling soon, sir," the gardener said. "We should empty the pool if we don't want any trouble with the pipes."

"Don't do it today," said Gatsby. He turned to me and said, "You know, old sport, I haven't used that pool all summer. Shall we go for a swim?"

I wanted to say yes. For some strange reason, I did not want to leave him alone. But it was past nine now and I had to take the train to work.

"I can't," I said. "But I'll call you today around noon."

"Do, old sport."

We shook hands and I walked away. But just before I reached the edge of his yard, I turned around.

"They're a bad crowd," I yelled at him across the lawn. "You're worth more than the whole bunch of them!"

I've always been glad I said that. It was the only praise I ever gave him. First he nodded politely, then his face broke into that beautiful, understanding smile of his.

"Goodbye," I called. "I enjoyed breakfast, Gatsby."

Chapter 15

Up in the city, I tried to do some work, but I fell asleep in my chair instead. The ringing telephone woke me up at around noon. It was Jordan Baker.

"I left Daisy's house," she said. "I'm at Hempstead now. You weren't so nice to me last night."

I knew she was right. But the truth was, I didn't really care.

"How could it have mattered?" I asked.

She was silent for a moment. Then she said, "However, I want to see you." She asked if we could meet that day, but I said no, I was busy.

There was no gladness in our words or voices. But we set a date to meet, and we both hung up the phone sharply.

I called Gatsby's house a few minutes later, but the line was busy. I tried four times, but each time, I couldn't get through. I decided to go home early, on the 3:50 p.m. train.

As I rode the train home, I looked out the window into the land of dust to see if there was still a crowd around Wilson's garage. I was surprised to find nobody there. Later on, I found out what happened after Tom, Jordan, and I left the sad scene the night before.

Myrtle's sister, Catherine, was called. She arrived after the body had been moved to a hospital. Some kind or curious person drove her there. After the police and the crowd had left, Michaelis sat with Wilson in the little office. Wilson didn't sleep through the night. He stared at the wall and would sometimes cry out, "Oh, my god!"

Toward dawn, Wilson started saying

strange things to Michaelis.

"I can find out whose yellow car that was," he whispered. Then he told Michaelis that a couple of months ago, his wife had come home with a broken nose. He then told Michaelis to open the top drawer of a desk in the office. When Michaelis opened it, he found a black leather dog leash.

"This? It's just a dog leash," said Michaelis.

Wilson stared and nodded.

"I found it yesterday. It was wrapped up in nice paper," said Wilson. He started rocking from side to side. "Then he killed her."

"Who did?"

"I'll find out," said Wilson.

"You're not making any sense," Michaelis said. "You're tired, George. Why don't you lay down here and try to get some sleep?"

"He killed her!"

"It was an accident, George," Michaelis said.

George Wilson shook his head. "I know!"

he said. "It was the man in that car. She ran out to speak to him and he wouldn't stop." Wilson's eyes turned toward the window, and he walked over to it. He leaned his head against the glass and said, "I told her. I told her she might trick me, but she couldn't trick God. I brought her here, to this window, and I showed her. I said, 'Look! God knows what you've been doing—everything you've been doing. You can't trick God!'"

Michaelis stared at Wilson, then joined him at the window. He realized with shock that Wilson was looking at the huge eyes of Doctor T. J. Eckleburg.

"That's just an advertisement, George," he said softly.

"God sees everything," repeated Wilson.

By 6 a.m. Michaelis was too tired to stay awake. He told Wilson he would be right across the street if he needed anything. Then he went home and went to sleep. Four hours later, Michaelis woke up and went over to

Wilson's to check on him. But Wilson was gone.

Later, the police were able to trace George Wilson's movement from the garage to Port Roosevelt, and then to Gad's Hill. He was on foot the whole time. At Gad's Hill he had bought a sandwich that he didn't eat. Some boys had seen him walking down the road. They told the police that he was "acting kind of crazy." By about 2:30 p.m., he was in West Egg. He asked someone the way to Gatsby's house. So by that time, he knew Gatsby's name.

At two o'clock, Gatsby put on his swimming suit and headed out to the pool. He had kept his telephone line open in case Daisy called, and that was why I couldn't get through to him. But Daisy never called. Perhaps he knew she wouldn't. And perhaps he no longer cared. I believe he went out to the pool that day feeling that he had lost his old, warm world. He had lived too long with a single dream, and now he was paying the price. He must have looked up at the sky and seen a world he didn't recognize.

One of the servants heard the shots, but he said he didn't realize what the sounds were. When I came rushing to Gatsby's house shortly afterward, I think we all knew something was wrong. The gardener, the servant, and I all hurried toward the pool. The wind was causing gentle little waves to dance all across the water. And in the middle of this floated Gatsby, trailing a thin red line of blood behind him.

It was when we were bringing Gatsby's body toward the house that the gardener noticed another body lying nearby in the grass. It was Wilson. He had shot himself too.

Chapter 16

Even now, two years later, I still remember the few days after Gatsby's death as an endless string of police questions. I was surprised to find that I was the only person who knew anything about Gatsby at all. I was even more surprised to find that I was the only person who seemed to care that he was dead.

I called Daisy half an hour after we found his body. But she and Tom had gone away that afternoon, taking many bags with them.

"Did they leave an address where they could be reached?" I asked their servant on the phone.

"No, sir."
"Did they say when they'd be back?"
"No."
"Do you have any idea where they are?"
"I don't know, sir."

I wanted to bring somebody to him—a friend, or someone he worked with, or an officer he knew in the war. Anybody would have been fine. I wanted to go into the room where his body lay and reassure him. I wanted to say, "Don't worry, Gatsby. I'll get somebody for you. I won't let you go through this alone." But there really was no one.

I couldn't reach Wolfsheim over the phone, so the next day I sent him a letter. I looked everywhere for Gatsby's parents' address but couldn't find anything. The only link to Gatsby's past was the picture of Dan Cody hanging on the wall.

It was on the third day after his death that a short letter from Minnesota arrived. It was signed Henry C. Gatz. It was Gatsby's father.

He said he was coming immediately and to please delay the funeral until he arrived.

Gatsby's father soon arrived. He was a thin, old man who looked almost helpless. He had on a long, cheap jacket, even in the warmth of September. He could not stop shaking, so I asked him to come inside and gave him some food. But he couldn't eat anything.

"I saw it in the Chicago newspaper," he said. "It was all in there. I came right away."

"I'm sorry," I said. "I didn't know how to reach you."

"The newspaper said it was a crazy man who shot him. He must have been very crazy."

"Would you like some coffee?" I asked.

"No, I'm fine, thank you," he said. "Where is Jimmy?"

I took him into the room where his son lay. I left him alone in there. After a while, Mr. Gatz came out, tears still rolling slowly down his cheeks. I tried to speak to him as softly as possible.

"I didn't know what kind of funeral you would like, Mr. Gatz," I said. "I thought you might want to take the body back West."

"Jimmy always liked it better here, in the East," Gatz said. "He rose up to his position in the East. He had a big future ahead of him. If he lived, he would have been a great man."

I said he must want some rest and showed him to a bedroom. He fell asleep immediately.

The morning of the funeral, I went to Wolfsheim's office in New York. He would, I thought, at the very least come to the funeral.

When I arrived at his office, a young woman answered the door and tried to turn me away.

"Nobody's here right now," she said roughly. "Try some other time."

But I could hear people behind her. I mentioned Gatsby's name and she changed her attitude.

"Oh, I'm sorry," she said. "Hold on." She brought Wolfsheim to the door, and he greeted me with open arms. He said it was a sad time for all of us and offered me a cigarette.

"I remember when I first met him," he said, lighting his cigarette. "He was so poor he didn't even have a change of clothes. He had to wear his army uniform everywhere. He came into a bar I was running and asked for a job. He hadn't eaten anything in a few days. I said, 'Come on, have some lunch with me.' So he sat down and ate four dollars worth of food in half an hour."

"Did you start him in the business?" I asked.

"Yes," he said. "I taught him everything."

"Now he's dead," I said after a moment. "You were his closest friend, so I know you will come to his funeral this afternoon."

Wolfsheim's eyes filled with tears. "I'd like to come," he said, "but I can't. The police and the law know who I am. I just can't go out there. They may know what kind of business

Gatsby was doing, and I can't get mixed up in it. I'm sorry, but it has to be that way."

"There's nothing to get mixed up in," I said. "He's dead. It's over now."

"I'm sorry," said Wolfsheim. He took my hand and shook it.

When I left Wolfsheim's office, the sky had turned dark and it was beginning to rain. When I arrived at Gatsby's house, I saw Mr. Gatz walking through the halls excitedly. His pride in his son and his wealth was increasing.

He came up to me and said he had something to show me. It was a photograph of Gatsby's house. The paper was bent at the corners from many hands touching it. I think he had shown it to people so often that it was more real to him now than the actual house itself.

"Jimmy sent me this picture," he said. "Look there, isn't it a very pretty picture?"

"Very pretty," I said. "Did you see him lately?"

"Jimmy came to see me two years ago. He bought me the house I live in now. We were very sad when he ran away from home, but now I see it was all for a reason. He knew he had a big future in front of him. And ever since he made his success, he was very generous with me."

Then he pulled something else out of his pocket. It was an old children's book.

"This was Jimmy's," he said. He opened the book to the last page and showed me a list written in pencil. It read:

SCHEDULE, SEPTEMBER 12, 1906

Rise from bed.....6 a.m.

Exercise.....6:15–6:30 a.m.

Study electricity, etc......7:15–8:15 a.m.

Work.....8:30–4:30 p.m.

Baseball and sports.....4:30–5:00 p.m.

Practice speaking and poise.....5:00–6:00 p.m.

Study.....7:00–9:00 p.m.

GOALS

No wasting time
No more smoking
Bath every other day
Read one book or magazine per week
Save $5.00 [crossed out] $3.00 per week
Be better to parents

A little before three o'clock, the minister came. I began to look out the window for arriving cars. So did Gatsby's father. We waited a while, then the servants gathered, and the minister said it was time to head out. Mr. Gatz said he worried the rain would keep people away. I took the minister aside and asked him to wait another half hour. But it was useless. Nobody came.

At the funeral, Gatsby was buried in the rain. And I remembered without anger or any emotion that Daisy never sent a letter or flowers.

Chapter 17

I see now that this has been a story about the West after all. Tom and Gatsby, Daisy and Jordan and I, we all came from the West. Perhaps we all lacked something that made us suitable for life in the East.

Even when the East excited me the most, things still felt a little wrong to me. There was too much action in the East, too much wealth, and too many people caring too little about each other. After Gatsby's death, I didn't want to live in the East anymore. So I decided to go home to the West.

I met Jordan Baker one last time. After the

night that Myrtle Wilson died, I knew I could never be with Jordan. She also knew then that it was over between us. But I didn't want to leave without saying sorry. She listened to me, but I don't think she forgave me.

One afternoon in late October, a few days before I left, I saw Tom Buchanan. He was walking ahead of me along Fifth Avenue. When he turned to look in a store window, he saw me, and I couldn't get away.

"What's the matter, Nick?" he asked, walking toward me with his hand out. "Don't you want to shake hands with me?"

"No, I don't," I said. "You know what I think of you."

"You're crazy, Nick," he said.

"Tom, what did you tell George Wilson that afternoon? I know he must have found you and talked to you. I know you must have given him Gatsby's name."

Tom stared at me, and I knew I had guessed correctly. As George Wilson walked through Long Island searching for the man with the yellow car, it was Tom who had told him the car was Gatsby's. I started to turn away, but Tom stopped me.

"I told him the truth," he said. "He came to my door while we were getting ready to leave. He tried to force his way in. He was crazy enough to kill me if I hadn't told him who owned the car. Anyway, Gatsby tricked us all! He was a criminal too, and he got what he deserved. He ran over Myrtle like he was running over a dog, and he never even stopped his car."

I was so shocked I didn't know what to say. Daisy hadn't told him the truth.

"That's not true," I managed to say.

"And I suffered too," said Tom. "After Myrtle died, I went to our apartment in the city. I saw her little dog sitting there, and I just cried like a baby. It was awful."

I could never forgive or like Tom. But I saw that in his mind, he had done nothing wrong. I realized finally that Tom and Daisy were careless people. They destroyed things and people and then just walked back into the safety of their money. They left other people to clean everything up. I gave up being angry and shook Tom's hand. I knew I would never see him again.

On my last night in Long Island, I went over to Gatsby's empty house. I looked at it one last time and then wandered down to the beach. I sat on the sand. I looked up at the stars and began to imagine Long Island as it would have looked to the first European sailors who saw it. Instead of Gatsby's house, there would have been trees here, and instead of a city, there would have been a forest. I thought about that old world, and I thought about Gatsby when he first saw the green light at the end of Daisy's dock. It was his discovery—he had finally come to a world where he could reach his dreams. What he didn't realize was that his dreams were always moving further into the past. But he kept reaching toward the future. And so do we all. As we continue to reach forward, we move further into the past.

Word List

- 語形が規則変化する語の見出しは原形で示しています。不規則変化語は本文中で使われている形になっています。
- 一般的な意味を紹介していますので、一部の語で本文で実際に使われている品詞や意味と合っていないことがあります。
- 品詞は以下のように示しています。

名名詞	代代名詞	形形容詞	副副詞	動動詞	助助動詞
前前置詞	接接続詞	間間投詞	冠冠詞	略略語	俗俗語
熟熟語	頭接頭語	尾接尾語	号記号	関関係代名詞	

A

- **about to** 《be –》まさに〜しようとしている、〜するところだ
- **accept** 動 ①受け入れる ②同意する、認める
- **accident** 名 ①(不慮の)事故、災難 ②偶然 by accident 偶然に
- **accuse** 動《– of 〜》〜(の理由)で告訴[非難]する
- **act** 動 ①行動する ②演じる
- **actor** 名 俳優、役者
- **actual** 形 実際の、現実の
- **actually** 副 実際に、本当に、実は
- **address** 名 住所、アドレス
- **admire** 動 感心する、賞賛する
- **admit** 動 認める、許可する、入れる
- **Adriatic Sea** アドリア海
- **advantage** 名 有利な点[立場]、強み、優越
- **adventure** 名 冒険
- **advertisement** 名 広告、宣伝
- **advice** 名 忠告、助言、意見
- **affair** 名 事柄、事件 have an affair 浮気をする
- **afford** 動《can –》〜することができる、〜する(経済的・時間的な)余裕がある
- **afterward** 副 その後、のちに
- **agree on** 〜について合意する
- **agree with** (人)に同意する
- **agreement** 名 ①合意、協定 ②一致
- **ah** 間《驚き・悲しみ・賞賛などを表して》ああ、やっぱり
- **ahead** 熟 ahead of 〜より先[前]に、〜に先んじて go ahead 先に行く、《許可を表す》どうぞ
- **air** 熟 air of 〜な雰囲気 out of thin air どこからともなく
- **alike** 形 よく似ている
- **alive** 熟 come alive 生き生きしてくる、活気づく
- **all** 熟 after all やはり、結局 all along 最初からずっと all by oneself

自分だけで, 独力で日 all day 一日中, 明けても暮れても all day long 一日中, 終 all of a sudden 突然, 前触れもなしに all one's life ずっと, 生まれてから all over 〜中で, 全体に亘って, 〜の至る所で, 全て終わって, もうだめで all over the world 世界中に all right 大丈夫で, よろしい, 申し分ない, わかった, 承知した all the time ずっと, いつも, その間ずっと over it all 全体にわたって That's all right. いいんですよ。

- **Allied forces** 連合軍, 同盟軍
- **alone** 熟 leave 〜 alone 〜をそっとしておく
- **along with** 〜と一緒に
- **although** 接 〜だけれども, 〜にもかかわらず, たとえ〜でも
- **America** 名 アメリカ《国名・大陸》
- **American** 形 アメリカ(人)の 名 アメリカ人
- **anger** 名 怒り
- **angrily** 副 怒って, 腹立たしげに
- **announce** 動 (人に)知らせる, 公表する
- **another** 熟 in one way or another あれこれと, どうにかして
- **anxious** 形 ①心配な, 不安な ②切望して
- **anxiously** 副 心配[切望]して
- **anybody** 代 ①《疑問文・条件節で》誰か ②《否定文で》誰も(〜ない) ③《肯定文で》誰でも anybody who 〜する人はだれでも
- **anymore** 副《通例否定文, 疑問文で》今はもう, これ以上, これから
- **anyone** 代 ①《疑問文・条件節で》誰か ②《否定文で》誰も(〜ない) ③《肯定文で》誰でも
- **anything else** ほかの何か
- **anyway** 副 ①いずれにせよ, ともかく ②どんな方法でも
- **anywhere** 副 どこかへ[に], どこにも, どこへも, どこにでも
- **apart** 副 ①ばらばらに, 離れて ②別にして, それだけで
- **apartment** 名 アパート
- **apologize** 動 謝る, わびる
- **appear** 動 現れる
- **approach** 動 ①接近する ②話を持ちかける
- **argue** 動 論じる, 議論する
- **argument** 名 議論, 論争
- **army officer** 陸軍士官[将校]
- **arrange** 動 ①並べる, 整える ②取り決める ③準備する, 手はずを整える
- **arrival** 名 ①到着 ②到達
- **as** 熟 as far as 〜と同じくらい遠く, 〜まで, 〜する限り(では) as if あたかも〜のように, まるで〜みたいに as long as 〜する以上は, 〜である限りは as much as 〜と同じだけ as soon as 〜するとすぐ, 〜するや否や as though あたかも〜のように, まるで〜みたいに as 〜 as ever 相変わらず, これまでのように as 〜 as possible できるだけ〜 be known as 〜として知られている just as (ちょうど)であろうとおり see 〜 as … 〜を…と考える
- **aside** 副 わきへ(に), 離れて aside from 〜は別として brush aside 払いのける, 無視する
- **ask 〜 if** 〜かどうか尋ねる
- **asleep** 形 眠って(いる状態の) fall asleep 眠り込む, 寝入る 副 眠って,

休止して
- **assume** 動 仮定する
- **attached** 形 付属した
- **attend** 動 出席する
- **attention** 名 ①注意, 集中 ②配慮
- **attitude** 名 態度
- **avenue** 名 《A-, Ave.》 ～通り, ～街
- **awake** 形 目が覚めて
- **award** 名 賞, 賞品
- **away** 熟 from far away 遠くから go away 立ち去る
- **awful** 形 ①ひどい, 不愉快な ②恐ろしい

B

- **backside** 名 背面
- **baked** 形 焼いた
- **Baker** 名 ベイカー《人名》
- **band** 名 楽団
- **bandage** 名 包帯
- **bar** 名 酒場, バー
- **bare** 形 裸の, むき出しの
- **baseball** 名 野球
- **bathroom** 名 ①浴室 ②手洗い, トイレ
- **bay** 名 湾, 入り江
- **bead** 数珠玉,《-s》ビーズ［のネックレス］
- **bear** 動 耐える
- **beat** 動 ①打つ, 鼓動する ②打ち負かす beat down 打ち破る
- **bed** 熟 go to bed 床につく, 寝る
- **bedroom** 名 寝室
- **beer** 名 ビール
- **before** 熟 the night before 前の晩
- **beg** 動 懇願する, お願いする I beg your pardon. ごめんなさい。失礼ですが。
- **beginning** 名 初め, 始まり
- **behind** 前 ①～の後ろに, ～の背後に ②～に遅れて, ～に劣って
- **bell** 名 ベル, 鈴, 鐘
- **bend** 動 曲がる, 曲げる 名 (道路の)カーブ
- **bent** 動 bend (曲がる)の過去, 過去分詞
- **beside** 前 ①～のそばに, ～と並んで ②～と比べると ③～とはずれて
- **bet** 動 賭ける
- **bit** 名 ①小片, 少量 ②《a –》少し, ちょっと bit of land《a –》わずかの土地 in a bit すぐに
- **bite** 動 かむ, かじる
- **blanket** 名 毛布
- **bleed** 動 出血する, 血を流す［流させる］
- **blind** 形 視覚障害がある, 目の不自由な
- **blood** 名 ①血, 血液 ②血統, 家柄
- **bloody** 形 血だらけの
- **blue** 熟 gas blue ガス・ブルー《空色の一種》
- **bone** 名 ①骨,《-s》骨格 ②《-s》要点, 骨組み
- **bored** 形 うんざりした, 退屈した
- **Boston** 名 ボストン《都市名》
- **bother** 動 悩ます, 困惑させる
- **bow** 動 (～に) お辞儀する
- **break into** ～に押し入る, 急に～する

- □ **break off** 中断する
- □ **break off with** 関係を断つ
- □ **breath** 名息, 呼吸
- □ **brick** 名レンガ
- □ **brief** 形短い時間の
- □ **bring out** (物)をとりだす, 引き出す, (新製品など)を出す
- □ **brush aside** 払いのける, 無視する
- □ **building** 名建物, 建造物, ビルディング
- □ **bunch** 名房, 束, 群れ a bunch of 1束の
- □ **burst** 名破裂, 爆発
- □ **bury** 動埋葬する, 埋める
- □ **business district** ビジネス[オフィス]街
- □ **businessmen** 名businessman(ビジネスマン)の複数
- □ **but** 熟 not only ~ but (also) … ~だけでなく…もまた nothing but ただ~だけ, ~にすぎない, ~のほかは何も…ない
- □ **butler** 名執事

C

- □ **call in** ~を呼ぶ, ~に立ち寄る
- □ **call on** 呼びかける, 招集する, 求める, 訪問する
- □ **call out** 叫ぶ, 呼び出す, 声を掛ける
- □ **call up** 電話で呼び出す
- □ **calm** 動静まる, 静める calm down 静まる
- □ **calmly** 副落ち着いて, 静かに
- □ **Camp Taylor** テイラー駐屯地
- □ **Can I ~?** ~してもよいですか。
- □ **can't help** 避けられない, ~せずにはいられない
- □ **careless** 形不注意な, うかつな
- □ **Carraway** 名キャラウェイ《人名》
- □ **carry into** ~の中に運び入れる
- □ **carry on** ①続ける ②持ち運ぶ
- □ **carry out** 外へ運び出す, [計画を]実行する
- □ **case** 熟 in case ~だといけないので, 念のため, 万が一
- □ **catch up to** ~に追いつく
- □ **Catherine** 名キャサリン《人名》
- □ **Catholic** 形カトリックの
- □ **caught** 熟 get caught up in ~に巻き込まれる
- □ **cent** 名セント《米国などの通貨単位。1ドルの100分の1》
- □ **central** 形中央の, 主要な
- □ **Central Park** セントラル・パーク《地名》
- □ **certain** 形 ①ある ②いくらかの
- □ **certainly** 副確かに, 必ず
- □ **champagne** 名シャンパン
- □ **chapter** 名(書物の)章
- □ **character** 名品性, 人格
- □ **charming** 形魅力的な, チャーミングな
- □ **chase** 動 ①追跡する, 追い[探し]求める ②追い立てる
- □ **cheat** 動だます, ごまかす
- □ **check on** ~を調べる
- □ **cheek** 名ほお
- □ **cheerful** 形上機嫌の, 元気のよい, (人を)気持ちよくさせる
- □ **cheerfully** 副元気に, 快活に
- □ **Chicago** 名シカゴ《都市名》

- ☐ **Chicago White Sox** シカゴ・ホワイトソックス《プロ野球チーム名》
- ☐ **cigarette** 名(紙巻)たばこ
- ☐ **circus** 名サーカス(団)
- ☐ **clearly** 副明らかに, はっきりと
- ☐ **clever** 形頭のよい, 利口な
- ☐ **close to** 《be –》～に近い
- ☐ **closely** 副①密接に ②念入りに, 詳しく
- ☐ **closet** 名戸棚, 物置, 押し入れ
- ☐ **coast** 名海岸, 沿岸
- ☐ **Cody** コーディー《人名》
- ☐ **coldly** 副冷たく, よそよそしく
- ☐ **colored** 形①色のついた ②有色人種の, 黒人の
- ☐ **come** 熟 come across ～に出くわす, ～に遭遇する come alive 生き生きしてくる, 活気づく come along ①一緒に来る, ついて来る ②やって来る, 現れる ③うまくいく, よくなる, できあがる come down ～を下りて来る, 田舎へ来る come in 中にはいる, やってくる, 出回る come into ～に入ってくる come on ①いいかげんにしろ, もうよせ, さあ来なさい ②(人)に偶然出会う come out 出てくる, 出掛ける, 姿を現す, 発行される come over やって来る, ～の身にふりかかる come through 成功する, 期待に沿う come up 近づいてくる, 階上に行く, 浮上する, 水面へ上ってくる, 発生する, 芽を出す come up with ～に追いつく, ～を思いつく, 考え出す, 見つけ出す there comes a point ～になることがある
- ☐ **comfortable** 形快適な, 心地いい
- ☐ **comfortably** 副心地よく, くつろいで
- ☐ **compared to** ～と比較して
- ☐ **complain** 動不平[苦情]を言う, ぶつぶつ言う I can't complain. ま, こんなもんだね。順調です。
- ☐ **completely** 副完全に, すっかり
- ☐ **Coney Island** コニー・アイランド《地域名。遊園地があった》
- ☐ **confident** 形自信のある, 自信に満ちた
- ☐ **confused** 形困惑した, 混乱した
- ☐ **connect** 動つながる, つなぐ, 関係づける
- ☐ **connection** 名つながり, 関係
- ☐ **contain** 動①含む, 入っている ②(感情などを)抑える
- ☐ **conversation** 名会話, 会談
- ☐ **correct** 形正しい, 適切な, りっぱな
- ☐ **correctly** 副正しく, 正確に
- ☐ **couch** 名長いす
- ☐ **could** 熟 could have done ～だったかもしれない《仮定法》 How could ～? 何だって～なんてことがありえようか? If＋《主語》＋could ～できればなあ《仮定法》
- ☐ **countryside** 名地方, 田舎
- ☐ **couple** 名①2つ, 対 ②夫婦, 一組 ③数個 a couple of 2, 3の
- ☐ **cover** 動覆う, 包む, 隠す be covered with ～でおおわれている
- ☐ **crazy** 形①狂気の, ばかげた, 無茶な ②夢中の, 熱狂的な
- ☐ **cream** 名クリーム 形クリーム(入り)の, クリーム色の
- ☐ **criminal** 名犯罪者, 犯人
- ☐ **criticize** 動①非難する, あら探しをする ②酷評する ③批評する
- ☐ **cross out** (文字を)線を引いて消す

- crowd 名 群集, 雑踏, 多数, 聴衆
- crowded 形 混雑した, 満員の
- cruel 形 残酷な, 厳しい
- crushed 形 押しつぶされた
- cry out 叫ぶ
- curiosity 名 ①好奇心 ②珍しい物 [存在]
- curious 形 好奇心の強い, 珍しい, 奇妙な, 知りたがる
- cut in 割り込む, 口を挟む
- cut off 切断する, 切り離す《be –》途絶する

D

- Daisy 名 デイジー《人名》
- Daisy Fay デイジー・フェイ《デイジーの旧姓時のフルネーム》
- damage 名 損害, 損傷
- damn 形 ひどい, とんでもない
- Dan Cody ダン・コーディー《人名》
- dancer 名 踊り子, ダンサー
- dark 熟 get dark 暗くなる
- darkening 形 だんだん暗くなる
- darkness 名 暗さ, 暗やみ
- date 熟 set a date 日取りを決める
- dawn 名 夜明け
- day 熟 all day 一日中, 明けても暮れても　all day long 一日中, 終日（過去の）ある日,（未来の）いつか　these days このごろ　in those days あのころは, 当時は
- deal 名 取引
- dearest 名 いとしい人《呼びかけ》
- death 名 死, 死ぬこと　sentenced to death《be –》死刑判決を受ける
- decade 名 10年間
- decision 名 ①決定, 決心 ②判決
- definitely 副 ①限定的に, 明確に, 確実に ②まったくそのとおり
- delay 動 遅らせる, 延期する
- delighted 形 喜んでいる
- deliver 動 配達する, 伝える
- demand 動 ①要求する, 尋ねる ②必要とする
- describe 動（言葉で）描写する, 特色を述べる, 説明する
- deserve 動（～を）受けるに足る, 値する,（～して）当然である
- desire 名 欲望, 欲求, 願望
- destroy 動 破壊する, 絶滅させる, 無効にする
- detail 名 ①細部,《-s》詳細 ②《-s》個人情報
- dig 動 ①掘る ②小突く ③探る
- dining room 食堂
- direct 動 ①指導する, 監督する ②（目・注意・努力などを）向ける
- direction 名 ①方向, 方角 ②《-s》指示, 説明書 ③指導, 指揮
- dirty 形 ①汚い, 汚れた ②卑劣な, 不正な
- disappear 動 見えなくなる, 姿を消す, なくなる
- disappointed 形 がっかりした, 失望した
- discomfort 名 不快（なこと）, 辛苦, つらさ
- discovery 名 発見
- dishonest 形 不誠実な
- dislike 動 嫌う
- distance 名 距離, 隔たり, 遠方

Word List 163

- **district** 名①地方, 地域 ②行政区
- **division** 名①分割 ②部門 ③境界 ④割り算
- **divorce** 動離婚する 名離婚, 分離
- **do with** ~を処理する
- **Do you mind if ... ?** ~したらお邪魔ですか
- **dock** 名ドック, 波止場, 埠頭
- **door** 熟 walk out the door ドアの外に出る, どこかに行く
- **doorway** 名戸口, 玄関, 出入り口
- **downstairs** 副階下で, 下の部屋で 名階下
- **dozen** 名1ダース, 12(個)
- **draw** 動引く, 引っ張る
- **drawer** 名引き出し
- **dreamy** 形夢を見る, 空想にふける
- **dress in white** 白い服を着る
- **drew** 動 draw (引く)の過去
- **drive ~ home** ~を車で家まで送る
- **drive away** 車で走り去る, 追い払う, 追い散らす
- **drive up** 車でやって来る
- **driver** 名①運転手 ②(馬車の)御者
- **drop the subject** 話題を打ち切る
- **drove** 動 drive (車で行く)の過去
- **drunk** 熟 get drunk 酔っ払う
- **dumb** 形①口のきけない ②物も言えない
- **dust** 名ちり, ほこり, ごみ, 粉
- **dusty** 形ほこりだらけの

E

- **each other** お互いに
- **each time** ~するたびに
- **eager to** 形《be – 》しきりに~したがっている
- **eagerly** 副熱心に, しきりに
- **earn** 動儲ける, 稼ぐ
- **easily** 副①容易に, たやすく, 苦もなく ②気楽に
- **Eckleburg** 名エクルバーグ《人名》
- **edge** 名①刃 ②端, 縁
- **educate** 動教育する, (~するように)訓練する
- **effort** 名努力(の成果)
- **either A or B** AかそれともB
- **electricity** 名電気
- **else** 熟 anything else ほかの何か
- **embarrassed** 形恥ずかしい, 当惑して
- **emotion** 名感激, 感動, 感情
- **empire** 名①帝国 ②大企業
- **end** 熟 at the end of ~の終わりに end up at 最後に~に行く
- **endless** 形終わりのない, 無限の
- **enemy** 名敵
- **engage** 動約束する, 婚約する
- **England** 名①イングランド ②英国
- **enough** 熟 have had enough of ~はもうたくさんだ
- **etc** 略 ~など, その他 (= et cetera)
- **Europe** 名ヨーロッパ
- **European** 名ヨーロッパ人 形ヨーロッパ(人)の
- **even though** ~であるけれども, ~にもかかわらず
- **ever** 熟 as ~ as ever 相変わらず, これまでのように ever since それ以

来ずっと
- **every other** 1つおきの〜
- **every time** 〜するときはいつも
- **everybody** 代 誰でも, 皆
- **everyday** 形 毎日の, 日々の
- **everyone** 代 誰でも, 皆
- **everything** 代 すべてのこと[もの], 何でも, 何もかも
- **everywhere** 副 どこにいても, いたるところに
- **evidence** 名 ①証拠, 証人 ②形跡
- **evil** 形 ①邪悪な ②有害な, 不吉な
- **example** 熟 fine example of 〜の好見本
- **exception** 名 例外, 除外, 異論
- **excited** 形 興奮した, わくわくした
- **excitedly** 副 興奮して
- **excitement** 名 興奮(すること)
- **exciting** 形 興奮させる, わくわくさせる
- **excuse oneself** 辞退する
- **exercise** 名 運動, 体操
- **expect** 動 予期[予測]する, (当然のこととして)期待する
- **explode** 動 ①爆発する[させる] ②(感情が)ほとばしる, 突然〜し出す
- **expression** 名 ①表現, 表示, 表情 ②言い回し, 語句
- **extra** 形 余分の, 臨時の
- **eye** 熟 take one's eyes off 〜から目をそらす

F

- **face to face** 面と向かって
- **fact** 熟 in fact つまり, 実は, 要するに
- **faint** 形 かすかな, 弱い, ぼんやりした
- **fall asleep** 眠り込む, 寝入る
- **fall in love** 恋におちる
- **fall on** 〜に降りかかる
- **fall over** 〜につまずく, 〜の上に倒れかかる
- **false** 形 うその, 間違った, にせの, 不誠実な
- **familiar** 形 ①親しい, 親密な ②《be – with 〜》〜に精通している ③普通の, いつもの, おなじみの
- **fancy** 形 ①装飾的な, 見事な ②法外な, 高級な
- **far** 熟 as far as 〜と同じくらい遠く, 〜まで, 〜する限り(では) far away 遠く離れて from far away 遠くから
- **farming** 名 農業
- **fashion** 名 ①流行, 方法, はやり ②流行のもの(特に服装)
- **fashionable** 形 ①流行の ②上流社会の
- **fat** 形 太った
- **fault** 名 過失, 誤り
- **fear** 名 ①恐れ ②心配, 不安
- **feeling** 動 feel(感じる)の現在分詞 名 ①感じ, 気持ち ②触感, 知覚 ③同情, 思いやり, 感受性
- **feet** 熟 jump to one's feet 飛び起きる to one's feet 両足で立っている状態に
- **fellow** 名 ①仲間, 同僚 ②人, やつ
- **Fifth Avenue** 五番街《地名》
- **filled with** 《be – 》〜でいっぱいになる
- **find out** 見つけ出す, 気がつく, 知る, 調べる, 解明する

- ☐ **fine example of** ～の好見本
- ☐ **finished** 形 ①終わった, 仕上がった ②もうだめになった
- ☐ **first** 熟 at first 最初は, 初めのうちは
- ☐ **fish** 動 釣りをする
- ☐ **fix** 動 ①固定する[させる] ②修理する ③決定する ④用意する, 整える fix on ～にくぎ付けになる
- ☐ **flash** 動 ①閃光を発する ②さっと動く, ひらめく
- ☐ **flat** 形 ①平らな ②しぼんだ, 空気の抜けた
- ☐ **float** 動 ①浮く, 浮かぶ ②漂流する ③(心に)浮かぶ ④《be -ing》(うわさなどが)広まる float around 出回る
- ☐ **fold** 動 折りたたむ
- ☐ **fool around with** (人と)浮気する
- ☐ **foot** 熟 on foot 歩いて
- ☐ **football** 名 (英国で)サッカー, (米国で)アメリカンフットボール
- ☐ **footstep** 名 足音, 歩み
- ☐ **force** 名 力, 勢い Allied forces 連合軍, 同盟軍
- ☐ **forgave** 動 forgive(許す)の過去
- ☐ **forgive** 動 許す, 免除する
- ☐ **forth** 副 前へ, 外へ
- ☐ **fortune** 名 ①富, 財産 ②幸運, 繁栄, チャンス
- ☐ **Forty-second Street** 四十二番街《地名》
- ☐ **forward** 副 ①前方に ②将来に向けて ③先へ, 進んで
- ☐ **France** 名 フランス《国名》
- ☐ **free** 熟 shake someone free ～を振り離す
- ☐ **full of** 《be -》～で一杯である
- ☐ **fun** 熟 make fun of ～を物笑いの種にする, からかう
- ☐ **funeral** 名 葬式, 葬列
- ☐ **funny** 形 ①おもしろい, こっけいな ②奇妙な, うさんくさい
- ☐ **furniture** 名 家具, 備品, 調度
- ☐ **further** 副 いっそう遠く, その上に, もっと

G

- ☐ **Gad's Hill** ギャッズ・ヒル《地名》
- ☐ **gamble** 動 賭ける, 賭け事をする
- ☐ **gambler** 名 賭博師, 相場師
- ☐ **gangster** 名 ギャング, 悪漢
- ☐ **garage** 名 (車の)車庫, 修理工場
- ☐ **gardener** 名 庭師, 園芸家
- ☐ **gas** 名 ガソリン
- ☐ **gas blue** ガス・ブルー《空色の一種》
- ☐ **gather** 動 集まる, 集める
- ☐ **Gatsby** 名 ギャツビー《人名》
- ☐ **Gatz** 名 ギャッツ《人名》
- ☐ **generous** 形 ①寛大な, 気前のよい ②豊富な
- ☐ **gentle** 形 ①優しい, 温和な ②柔らかな
- ☐ **George B. Wilson** ジョージ・B・ウィルソン《人名》
- ☐ **German** 形 ドイツ(人・語)の 名 ①ドイツ人 ②ドイツ語
- ☐ **Germany** 名 ドイツ《国名》
- ☐ **get** 熟 get away 逃げる, 逃亡する, 離れる get caught up in ～に巻き込まれる get dark 暗くなる get drunk 酔っ払う get home 家に着く[帰る]

get into ～に入る, 入り込む, ～に巻き込まれる get mixed up かかわり合いになる, 巻き添えを食う get off (～から)降りる get on (電車などに)乗る, 気が合う get out ①外に出る, 出て行く, 逃げ出す ②取り出す, 抜き出す get out of ～から下車する, ～から取り出す, ～から外へ出る[抜け出る] get ready 用意[支度]をする get stiff 硬直する get through 乗り切る, ～を通り抜ける get up 起き上がる, 立ち上がる get up to ～まで行く, ～しようと立ち上がる

- **ghost** 名 幽霊
- **give ~ a long look** ～をじっと見つめる
- **give up** あきらめる, やめる, 引き渡す give up on ～に見切りをつける
- **gladness** 名 喜ばしさ
- **glow** 動 ①(火が)白熱して輝く ②(体が)ほてる
- **go** 熟 go ahead 先に行く,《許可を表す》どうぞ go away 立ち去る go for ～に出かける, ～を追い求める, ～を好む go for a walk 散歩に行く go home 帰宅する go in 中に入る, 開始する go into ～に入る, (仕事)に就く go on 続く, 続ける, 進み続ける, 起こる, 発生する go out 外出する, 外へ出る go over ～を越えて行く, ～へ渡る go over to ～の前に[へ]行く, ～に出向いて行く go through 通り抜ける go through with (計画を)遂行する go to bed 床につく, 寝る go to sleep 寝る go up ～に近づく go with ～と一緒に行く, ～と調和する, ～にとても似合う let go 解雇する let go of ～から手を離す
- **God** 熟 Oh, My God! 何てことだ!

- **gold** 名 金, 金貨, 金製品, 金色 形 金の, 金製の, 金色の
- **golden** 形 ①金色の ②金製の
- **golf** 名 ゴルフ
- **golfer** 名 ゴルファー
- **goodness** 名 善良さ, よいところ
- **got to** ～しなければならない
- **government** 名 政治, 政府, 支配
- **grab** 動 ふいにつかむ, ひったくる
- **grain** 名 穀物, 穀類 grain liquor グレイン・アルコール(エチルアルコール)
- **grand** 形 雄大な, 壮麗な
- **grass** 名 草, 芝生
- **Greek** 形 ギリシャ(人・語)の 名 ①ギリシャ人 ②ギリシャ語
- **greet** 動 ①あいさつする ②(喜んで)迎える
- **grow up** 成長する, 大人になる
- **guess at** ～を推測する
- **guest** 名 客, ゲスト

H

- **haircut** 名 散髪
- **haired** 形 頭髪が～の
- **hall** 名 公会堂, ホール, 大広間, 玄関
- **ham** 名 ハム
- **hand** 熟 hand out 配る put ～ in one's hands ～を…に預ける shake hands 握手をする with one's open hand 平手で
- **handsome** 形 端正な(顔立ちの), りっぱな, (男性が)ハンサムな
- **hang** 動 かかる, かける, つるす, ぶら下がる hang around (あてもなく)う

- ろうろうする　hang on ～につかまる、しがみつく、がんばる、(電話を)切らずに待つ　hang up つるす、電話を切る
- **happily** 副 幸福に、楽しく、うまく、幸いにも
- **happiness** 名 幸せ、喜び
- **hard mouth** 口が堅い
- **hard to** ～し難い
- **hardly** 副 ①ほとんど～でない、わずかに　②厳しく、かろうじて
- **harm** 名 害、損害、危害
- **hate** 動 嫌う、憎む、(～するのを)いやがる
- **have** 熟 could have done ～だったかもしれない《仮定法》have an affair 浮気をする　have had enough of ～はもうたくさんだ　have no idea わからない　have to do with ～と関係がある　should have done ～すべきだった(のにしなかった)《仮定法》would have … if ～ もし～だったとしたら…しただろう
- **head home** 家に帰る
- **hear of** ～について聞く
- **heat** 名 熱、暑さ
- **hell** 名 地獄、地獄のようなところ[状態]
- **help** 熟 can't help 避けられない、～せずにはいられない
- **helpless** 形 無力の、自分ではどうすることもできない
- **helplessly** 副 どうすることもできず
- **Hempstead** 名 ヘムステッド《地名》
- **hen** 名 雌鳥
- **Henry C. Gatz** ヘンリー・C・ギャッツ《人名》
- **here** 熟 here and there あちこちで　Look here. ほら。ねえ。
- **hey** 間 ①《呼びかけ・注意を促して》おい、ちょっと　②へえ、おや、まあ
- **hid** 動 hide (隠れる)の過去、過去分詞
- **hidden** 形 隠れた
- **hide** 動 隠れる、隠す、隠れて見えない、秘密にする
- **hire** 動 雇う、賃借りする
- **hired** 形 雇入れの
- **Hold on.** お待ちください。
- **hold onto** ～にしがみつく
- **hold out** ①差し出す、(腕を)伸ばす　②持ちこたえる、粘る、耐える
- **hold up** ①維持する、支える　②～を持ち上げる　③(指を)立てる
- **home** 熟 drive ～ home ～を車で家まで送る　get home 家に着く[帰る]　go home 帰宅する　head home 家に帰る
- **honest** 形 ①正直な、誠実な、心からの　②公正な、感心な
- **honor** 動 尊敬する、栄誉を与える
- **horn** 名 (車の)クラクション、ホーン
- **host** 名 ①客をもてなす主人　②(テレビなどの)司会者
- **How** 熟 How about ～? ～はどうですか。～しませんか。　How could ～? 何だって～なんてことがありえようか?　How do you like ～? ～はどう思いますか。～はいかがですか。　how to ～する方法　no matter how どんなに～であろうとも
- **however** 副 たとえ～でも 接 けれども、だが
- **huge** 形 巨大な、ばく大な

- □ **hung** 動 hang（かかる）の過去, 過去分詞
- □ **hurry down** 急いで下りる[駆け込む]
- □ **hurry over** ～を慌ててやる

I

- □ **I beg your pardon.** ごめんなさい。失礼ですが。もう一度言ってください。
- □ **I do not mean to** ～するつもりはないのですが
- □ **idea** 熟 have no idea わからない
- □ **if** 熟 as if あたかも～のように, まるで～みたいに ask ~ if ～かどうか尋ねる if necessary もし必要ならば If +《主語》+ could ～できればなあ《仮定法》 see if ～かどうかを確かめる what if もし～だったらどうなるだろうか wonder if ～ではないかと思う would have … if ~ もし～だったとしたら…しただろう
- □ **illegal** 形 違法な, 不法な
- □ **imagine** 動 想像する, 心に思い描く
- □ **immediately** 副 すぐに, ～するやいなや
- □ **importance** 名 重要性, 大切さ
- □ **including** 前 ～を含めて, 込みで
- □ **increase** 動 増加[増強]する, 増やす, 増える
- □ **independent** 形 独立した, 自立した
- □ **insist** 動 ①主張する, 断言する ②要求する
- □ **instantly** 副 すぐに, 即座に
- □ **instead** 副 その代わりに
- □ **intend** 動《- to ~》～しようと思う, ～するつもりである
- □ **interested** 形 興味を持った, 関心のある
- □ **interesting** 形 おもしろい, 興味を起こさせる
- □ **introduction** 名 紹介, 導入
- □ **invitation** 名 招待（状）, 案内（状）
- □ **It is ~ for someone to …** （人）が…するのは～だ
- □ **It takes two people to** ～するには2人必要
- □ **itself** 代 それ自体, それ自身

J

- □ **jacket** 名 短い上着
- □ **James Gatz** ジェイムズ・ギャッツ《人名》
- □ **Jay Gatsby** ジェイ・ギャツビー《人名》
- □ **jealousy** 名 嫉妬, ねたみ
- □ **Jimmy** 名 ジミー《Jamesの愛称》
- □ **Jordan Baker** ジョーダン・ベイカー《人名》
- □ **judge** 動 判断する, 評価する
- □ **jump out of** ～から飛び出す
- □ **jump to one's feet** 飛び起きる
- □ **jump up** 素早く立ち上がる
- □ **just as** （ちょうど）であろうとおり
- □ **just then** そのとたんに

K

- □ **Kaiser Wilhelm** ヴィルヘルム皇

帝(1859–1941)《ドイツ皇帝》
- **keep out of** ～を避ける, ～に干渉しない
- **kind of** ある程度, いくらか, ～のような物[人]
- **kiss** 動 キスする
- **knee** 名 ひざ
- **knock** 動 ノックする, たたく, ぶつける knock over 張り倒す 名 打つこと, 戸をたたくこと[音]
- **know** 熟 you know ご存知のとおり, そうでしょう
- **known as** 《be –》～として知られている

L

- **lack** 動 不足している, 欠けている
- **Lake Superior** スペリオル湖
- **land** 熟 bit of land《a –》わずかの土地
- **lap** 名 ひざ
- **lately** 副 近ごろ, 最近
- **later** 熟 later on もっと後で, のちほど sooner or later 遅かれ早かれ
- **laughter** 名 笑い(声)
- **lawn** 名 芝生
- **lay** 動 ①置く, 横たえる, 敷く ②整える ③lie(横たわる)の過去 lay down 下に置く, 横たえる
- **lead a life** 生活を送る, 暮らす
- **lean** 動 ①もたれる, 寄りかかる ②傾く, 傾ける lean back 後ろにもたれる lean over ～にかがみ込む
- **leash** 名 (動物をつなぐ)皮ひも, 鎖
- **least** 名 最小, 最少 at least 少なくとも
- **leather** 名 皮革, 皮製品
- **leave ~ alone** ～をそっとしておく
- **leave for** ～に向かって出発する
- **led** 動 lead(導く)の過去, 過去分詞
- **lemon** 名 レモン
- **less** 形 ～より小さい[少ない] 副 ～より少なく, ～ほどでなく
- **let go** 解雇する
- **let go of** ～から手を離す
- **level** 名 ①水平, 平面 ②水準 low level of ～の下層
- **lie** 動 ①うそをつく ②横たわる, 寝る ③(ある状態に)ある, 存在する lie down 横たわる, 横になる lie nearby すぐ近くに位置する 名 うそ
- **life** 熟 all one's life ずっと, 生まれてから lead a life 生活を送る, 暮らす
- **lightly** 副 軽く, そっと
- **like** 熟 would like ～がほしい would like to ～したいと思う Would you like ~? ～はいかがですか。
- **line of** ～の系統, 血筋
- **link** 名 結びつけるもの
- **lip** 名 唇,《-s》口
- **liquor** 名 (強い)酒, 蒸留酒 grain liquor グレイン・アルコール(エチルアルコール)
- **list** 名 名簿, 目録, 一覧表
- **listener** 名 聞く人, ラジオ聴取者
- **lit** 動 light(火をつける)の過去, 過去分詞
- **lively** 形 ①元気のよい, 活発な ②鮮やかな, 強烈な, 真に迫った
- **living room** 居間
- **locate** 動 置く, 居住する[させる]

- **loneliness** 名 孤独
- **lonely** 形 ①孤独な, 心さびしい ②ひっそりした, 人里離れた
- **long** 熟 all day long 一日中, 終日　as long as ～する以上は, ～である限りは　no longer もはや～でない[～しない]
- **Long Island** ロング・アイランド《地名》
- **look** 熟 give ～ a long look ～をじっと見つめる　look around まわりを見回す　look away 横を向く　look down 見下ろす　look down at ～に目[視線]を落とす　look for ～を探す　Look here. ほら。ねえ。　look in 中を見る, 立ち寄る　look on 傍観する, 眺める　look out ①外を見る ②気をつける, 注意する　look over ～越しに見る, ～を見渡す　look up 見上げる, 調べる
- **loudly** 副 大声で, 騒がしく
- **Louisville** 名 ルイヴィル《都市名》
- **love** 熟 be in love with ～に恋して, ～に心を奪われて　fall in love 恋におちる
- **lovely** 形 愛らしい, 美しい, すばらしい
- **lover** 名 ①愛人, 恋人 ②愛好者
- **low level of** ～の下層
- **lower** 形 もっと低い, 下級の, 劣った
- **lying** 動 lie (横たわる) の現在分詞

M

- **made of** 《be –》～でできて[作られて]いる
- **Madison Avenue** マディソン街《街路名》
- **maid** 名 お手伝い, メイド
- **main** 形 主な, 主要な
- **make** 熟 make fun of ～を物笑いの種にする, からかう　make into ～を…に仕立てる　make one's way 進む, 行く, 成功する　make sure 確かめる, 確認する　make way 道を譲る[あける], 前進する
- **manage** 動 ①動かす, うまく処理する ②経営[管理]する, 支配する ③どうにか～する
- **manner** 名 ①方法, やり方 ②態度, 様子 ③《-s》行儀, 作法, 生活様式
- **mansion** 名 大邸宅
- **many** 熟 so many 非常に多くの
- **marriage** 名 結婚(生活・式)
- **married** 動 marry (結婚する) の過去, 過去分詞　形 結婚した, 既婚の
- **marry** 動 結婚する
- **mass** 名 固まり, (密集した) 集まり
- **matter** 熟 matter to ～にとって重要である　not matter 問題にならない　no matter how どんなに～であろうとも　What's the matter? どうしたんですか。
- **McKee** 名 マッキー《人名》
- **mean** 熟 I do not mean to ～するつもりはないのですが　形 意地悪な
- **mean-looking** 形 意地悪そうな
- **meanwhile** 副 それまでの間, 一方では
- **medicine business** 薬業界
- **meeting** 動 meet (会う) の現在分詞　名 ①集まり, ミーティング, 面会 ②競技会
- **memory** 名 記憶(力), 思い出

- **mention** 動（〜について）述べる, 言及する
- **menu** 名メニュー, 献立表
- **metal** 名金属, 合金
- **Metropole** 名メトロポール《店名》
- **Meyer Wolfsheim** マイヤー・ウォルフシェム《人名》
- **Michaelis** 名マイケリス《人名》
- **mid** 形中央の, 中間の
- **middle** 名中間, 最中
- **midnight** 名夜の12時, 真夜中, 暗黒
- **Midwest** 名（アメリカ）中西部
- **might** 助《mayの過去》〜かもしれない
- **mild** 形柔和な, 温和な, 口あたりのよい, 穏やかな
- **mile** 名①マイル《長さの単位。1,609m》②《-s》かなりの距離
- **military** 形軍隊［軍人］の, 軍事の
- **milky white** 乳白色
- **mind** 名①心, 精神, 考え ②知性 動①気にする, いやがる ②気をつける, 用心する
- **minister** 名聖職者
- **Minnesota** 名ミネソタ《州名》
- **minute** 熟 in a minute すぐに
- **mirror** 名鏡
- **mix** 動①混ざる, 混ぜる ②（〜を）一緒にする
- **mixed** 熟 get mixed up かかわり合いになる, 巻き添えを食う
- **moment** 名①瞬間, ちょっとの間 ②（特定の）時, 時期 for a moment 少しの間 in a moment ただちに
- **Montenegro** 名モンテネグロ《国名》
- **morning** 熟 one morning ある朝
- **motor-boat** 名モーターボート
- **mouth** hard mouth 口が堅い
- **move around** あちこち移動する
- **move away** ①立ち去る ②移す, 動かす
- **move on** 先に進む
- **move to** 〜に引っ越す
- **movement** 名①動き, 運動 ②《-s》行動
- **much** 熟 as much as 〜と同じだけ too much of あまりに〜過ぎる
- **muscle** 名筋肉, 腕力
- **musical** 形音楽の
- **musician** 名音楽家
- **Myrtle Wilson** マートル・ウィルソン《人名》
- **mystery** 名①神秘, 不可思議 ②推理小説, ミステリー

N

- **name after** 〜にちなんで名付ける
- **narrow** 動狭くなる［する］
- **nearby** 副近くで, 間近で lie nearby すぐ近くに位置する
- **neatly** 副きちんと, 巧妙に
- **necessary** 形必要な, 必然の if necessary もし必要ならば
- **neighborhood** 名近所（の人々）, 付近
- **neither** 形どちらの〜も…でない neither 〜 nor … 〜も…もない 代（2者のうち）どちらも〜でない
- **New Haven** ニューヘーブン《地名》

- **New Orleans** ニューオーリンズ《地名》
- **New York** ニューヨーク《州名, 都市名》
- **New York City** ニューヨーク市《都市名》
- **newly** 副再び, 最近, 新たに
- **news** 名報道, ニュース, 便り, 知らせ
- **newspaper** 名新聞(紙)
- **Nick** 名ニック《人名》
- **night before** 《the-》前の晩
- **no longer** もはや～でない[～しない]
- **no matter how** どんなに～であろうとも
- **no one** 誰も[一人も]～ない
- **nobody** 代誰も[1人も]～ない
- **nod** 動うなずく, うなずいて～を示す
- **noise** 名騒音, 騒ぎ, 物音
- **nor** 接～もまたない neither ～ nor … ～も…もない
- **North Dakota** ノースダコタ《州名》
- **not matter** 問題にならない
- **not only ～ but (also) …** ～だけでなく…もまた
- **note** 名メモ, 覚え書き
- **nothing but** ただ～だけ, ～にすぎない, ～のほかは何も…ない
- **notice** 動気づく, 認める
- **now that** 今や～だから, ～からには
- **nowhere** 副どこにも～ない

O

- **offer** 動申し出る, 申し込む, 提供する
- **officer** 名陸軍士官[将校]
- **Oh, My God!** 何てことだ！
- **oil business** 石油産業
- **old sport** 《呼びかけで》君, 親友
- **one** 熟 one by one 1つずつ, 1人ずつ one day (過去の)ある日, (未来の)いつか one morning ある朝 this one これ, こちら
- **158th Street** 158番街《地名》
- **oneself** 熟 all by oneself 自分だけで, 独力で by oneself 一人で, 自分だけで, 独力で excuse oneself 辞退する for oneself 独力で, 自分のために
- **only** 熟 not only ～ but (also) … ～だけでなく…もまた
- **onto** 前～の上へ[に]
- **open** 熟 out in the open 明るみに出て
- **open hand** 平手
- **opportunity** 名好機, 適当な時期[状況]
- **opposite** 形反対の, 向こう側の
- **orchestra** 名管弦楽団, オーケストラ
- **other** 熟 every other 1つおきの～
- **ought** 助《- to ～》当然～すべきである, きっと～するはずである
- **out in the open** 明るみに出て
- **out of thin air** どこからともなく
- **over** 熟 all over ～中で, 全体に亘って, ～の至る所で, 全て終わって, もうだめで be over 終わる over and

over 何度も繰り返して　over it all 全体にわたって　over there あそこに
- **owe** 動 ①(〜を)負う, (〜を人の)お陰とする ②(金を)借りている, (人に対して〜の)義務がある
- **own** 熟 of one's own 自分自身の
- **owner** 名 持ち主, オーナー
- **Oxford** 名 オックスフォード《都市名, 大学名》Oxford man オックスフォード大学出身者[卒業生]

P

- **pack** 動 荷造りする, 詰め込む
- **package** 名 包み, パッケージ
- **paid** 動 pay(払う)の過去, 過去分詞
- **painful** 形 ①痛い, 苦しい, 痛ましい ②骨の折れる, 困難な
- **pair** 名 (2つから成る)一対, 一組, ペア
- **pale** 形 (顔色・人が)青ざめた, 青白い
- **pardon** 熟 I beg your pardon. ごめんなさい。失礼ですが
- **party** 熟 throw a party パーティーを開く
- **parent** 名 ①《-s》両親 ②先祖
- **pass around** 順に回す
- **pass down** (次の世代に)伝える
- **passing** 名 通行, 通過
- **passion** 名 情熱, (〜への)熱中
- **past** 形 過去の, この前の 名 過去(の出来事) 前 《時間・場所》〜を過ぎて, 〜を越して 副 通り越して, 過ぎて
- **path** 名 ①(踏まれてできた)小道, 歩道 ②進路, 通路
- **pause** 名 ①(活動の)中止, 休止 ②区切り 動 休止する, 立ち止まる
- **pay** 動 支払う, 払う, 報いる
- **pearl** 名 真珠
- **peel** 名 (果物などの)皮
- **Pennsylvania Station** ペンシルベニア駅
- **people** 熟 It takes two people to 〜するには2人必要
- **per** 前 〜につき, 〜ごとに
- **perfectly** 副 完全に, 申し分なく
- **perfume** 名 香水
- **perhaps** 副 たぶん, ことによると
- **personal** 形 個人の, 私的な
- **pet** 動 やさしくなでる, かわいがる
- **Philadelphia** 名 フィラデルフィア《都市名》
- **photo** 名 写真
- **photograph** 名 写真 動 写真を撮る
- **photographer** 名 写真家, カメラマン
- **physically** 副 ①自然法則上, 物理的に ②肉体的に, 身体的に
- **pick out** 拾い出す, えり抜く, 選び出す
- **pick up** 拾い上げる, 車で迎えに行く, 習得する, 再開する, 回復する
- **pile** 名 積み重ね, (〜の)山
- **pipe** 名 管, 筒, パイプ
- **plate** 名 (浅い)皿
- **player** 名 ①競技者, 選手, 演奏者, 俳優 ②演奏装置
- **Plaza Hotel** プラザホテル
- **pleasantly** 副 楽しく, 心地よく
- **plenty** 名 十分, たくさん, 豊富

- **plus** 副 その上に, さらに
- **pm** 略 午後(= post meridiem)
- **point** 熟 at some point どこかの時点で　at this point 現在のところ　point out 指し示す, 指摘する, 目を向ける, 目を向けさせる　there comes a point ～になることがある
- **poise** 名 振る舞い
- **policeman** 名 警察官
- **politely** 副 ていねいに, 上品に
- **politician** 名 政治家, 政略家
- **pool** 名 プール
- **pop up** (不意に)現れる
- **porch** 名 ポーチ, 玄関, 車寄せ
- **port** 名 港, 港町
- **Port Roosevelt** ポート・ルーズヴェルト《地名》
- **position** 名 位置, 場所, 姿勢
- **possible** 形 ①可能な ②ありうる, 起こりうる　as ～ as possible できるだけ～
- **possibly** 副 ①あるいは, たぶん ②《否定文, 疑問文で》どうしても, できる限り, とても, なんとか
- **pour** 動 ①注ぐ, 浴びせる ②流れ出る, 流れ込む ③ざあざあ降る
- **powder** 名 粉末, おしろい
- **powerful** 形 力強い, 実力のある, 影響力のある
- **praise** 名 賞賛
- **precious** 形 貴重な, 高価な
- **press** 動 圧する, 押す
- **price** 名 値段, 代価
- **pride** 名 誇り, 自慢, 自尊心
- **prison** 名 ①刑務所, 監獄 ②監禁
- **private** 形 ①私的な, 個人の ②民間の, 私立の ③内密の, 人里離れた
- **probably** 副 たぶん, あるいは
- **professional** 形 専門の, プロの, 職業的な
- **proud** 形 ①自慢の, 誇った, 自尊心のある ②高慢な, 尊大な
- **prove** 動 ①証明する ②(～であることが)わかる, (～と)なる
- **pull off** 離れる, 去る, (衣服などを)脱ぐ
- **pull out** 引き抜く, 引き出す, 取り出す
- **pull up** 引っ張り上げる
- **puppy** 名 子犬
- **purple** 形 紫色の
- **push around** いじめる, 手荒に扱う
- **push someone out of** (人)を～からたたき出す
- **put ～ in one's hands** ～を…に預ける
- **put in** ～の中に入れる
- **put on** ①～を身につける, 着る ②～を…の上に置く
- **puzzle** 動 当惑させる, まごつかせる

Q

- **quickly** 副 敏速に, 急いで
- **quietly** 副 ①静かに ②平穏に, 控えめに
- **quite often** 頻繁に

R

- **race** 熟 white race 白色人種
- **raise** 動 ①上げる, 高める ②起こす

③~を育てる
- **rang** 動 ring (鳴る) の過去
- **rapidly** 副 速く, 急速, すばやく, 迅速に
- **rather** 副 ①むしろ, かえって ②かなり, いくぶん, やや ③それどころか逆に would rather ~する方がよい
- **reach out** 手を伸ばす
- **reach over** 手を伸ばす
- **read out** 声を出して読む, 読み上げる
- **read over** ~に目を通す
- **ready** 熟 be ready to すぐに [いつでも] ~できる, ~する構えで get ready 用意 [支度] をする
- **reality** 名 現実, 実在, 真実 (性)
- **realize** 動 理解する, 実現する
- **reason** 熟 for some reason なんらかの理由で, どういうわけか
- **reassure** 動 安心させる
- **recent** 形 近ごろの, 近代の
- **recognize** 動 認める, 認識 [承認] する
- **Red Cross** 赤十字社
- **refuse** 動 拒絶する, 断る
- **relate** 動 関連がある, かかわる
- **relax** 動 ①くつろがせる ②ゆるめる, 緩和する
- **remain** 動 ①残っている, 残る ②(~の) ままである [いる]
- **remaining** 形 残った, 残りの
- **remark** 名 意見, 記事, 批評
- **remind** 動 思い出させる, 気づかせる
- **remove** 動 取り去る, 除去する
- **rent** 動 賃借りする
- **repair** 動 修理 [修繕] する 名 修理, 修繕
- **repeat** 動 繰り返す
- **replace** 動 ①取り替える, 差し替える ②元に戻す
- **reply** 動 答える, 返事をする, 応答する
- **request** 名 願い, 要求 (物), 需要
- **respect** 動 尊敬 [尊重] する
- **respond** 動 答える, 返答 [応答] する
- **response** 名 応答, 反応, 返答
- **ridden** 動 ride (乗る) の過去分詞
- **riding clothes** 乗馬服
- **right** 熟 all right 大丈夫で, よろしい, 申し分ない, わかった, 承知した right away すぐに right now 今すぐに, たった今 right then and there その瞬間にその場で That's all right. いいんですよ。
- **ring** 名 ①指輪 ②ベルの音 動 鳴る, 鳴らす
- **rip** 動 引き裂く, 切り裂く, 破る
- **Rise of the Colored Empires, The** 『有色帝国の隆盛』《書名》
- **rise up to** ~に浮かび上がる
- **risen** 動 rise (昇る) の過去分詞
- **roar with laughter** 大笑いをする, 爆笑する
- **robe** 名 ローブ, 化粧着, 部屋着
- **rode** 動 ride (乗る) の過去
- **roll** 動 転がる, 転がす roll down 転がり落ちる
- **Rolls Royce** ロールスロイス《車種名》
- **Rosy Rosenthal** ロージー・ローゼンタール《人名》

- □ **rough** 形 ①(手触りが)粗い ②荒々しい, 未加工の
- □ **roughly** 副 ①おおよそ, 概略的に, 大ざっぱに ②手荒く, 粗雑に
- □ **row** 動 (舟を)こぐ
- □ **rowboat** 名 (手こぎの)ボート
- □ **rude** 形 粗野な, 無作法な, 失礼な
- □ **ruin** 動 破滅させる
- □ **rumor** 名 うわさ
- □ **run** 熟 run away from 〜から逃れる run down 走って行く, 追いかけて捕まえる, 追い詰める, 狩り出す run into (思いがけず) 〜に出くわす run out 走り出る run over 一走りする, 〜の上を走る, ひき[押し]倒す run through 走り抜ける
- □ **rush** 動 突進する, せき立てる rush into 〜に突入する, 〜に駆けつける, 〜に駆け込む rush through さっさと終わらせる 名 殺到

S

- □ **safety** 名 安全, 無事, 確実
- □ **sailor** 名 船員, (ヨットの)乗組員
- □ **San Francisco** サンフランシスコ《米国の都市》
- □ **sand** 名 ①砂 ②《-s》砂漠, 砂浜
- □ **Santa Barbara** サンタ・バーバラ《都市名》
- □ **Saturday Evening Post, The** サタデー・イブニング・ポスト《雑誌名》
- □ **scandal** 名 スキャンダル, 醜聞
- □ **scared** 形 おびえた, びっくりした
- □ **schedule** 名 予定, スケジュール
- □ **search** 動 捜し求める, 調べる
- □ **secret** 名 秘密, 神秘
- □ **see** 熟 see if 〜かどうかを確かめる See you. ではまた。 see 〜 as … 〜を…と考える you see あのね, いいですか
- □ **seek** 動 捜し求める, 求める
- □ **seem** 動 (〜に)見える, (〜のように)思われる seem to be 〜であるように思われる
- □ **selection** 名 選択(物), 選抜, 抜粋
- □ **self-control** 名 セルフコントロール, 自制心
- □ **selfish** 形 わがままな, 自分本位の, 利己主義の
- □ **send for** 〜を呼びにやる, 〜を呼び寄せる
- □ **sense** 名 意味
- □ **sentence** 名 ①文 ②判決, 宣告 動 判決を下す, 宣告する sentenced to death《be -》死刑判決を受ける
- □ **separate** 動 ①分ける, 分かれる, 隔てる ②別れる, 別れさせる 形 分かれた, 別れた, 別々の
- □ **series** 名 一続き, 連続, シリーズ
- □ **serious** 形 ①まじめな, 真剣な ②重大な, 深刻な, (病気などが)重い
- □ **seriously** 副 ①真剣に, まじめに ②重大に
- □ **servant** 名 召使, 使用人, しもべ
- □ **serve** 動 ①仕える, 奉仕する ②(客の)応対をする, 給仕する, 食事[飲み物]を出す ③(役目を)果たす, 務める, 役に立つ
- □ **set a date** 日取りを決める
- □ **set up** 仕掛ける
- □ **sh** 間 しっ！, 静かに！
- □ **shade** 名 ①陰, 日陰 ②日よけ
- □ **shadow** 名 ①影, 暗がり ②亡霊

- **shake** 動 ①振る, 揺れる, 揺さぶる, 震える ②動揺させる shake hands 握手をする shake someone free ～を振り離す
- **Shall we ～?** (一緒に) ～しましょうか。
- **shame** 名 恥, 恥辱
- **shape** 名 ①形, 姿, 型 ②状態, 調子 動 形づくる, 具体化する
- **sharply** 副 鋭く, 激しく, はっきりと
- **shelf** 名 棚
- **shining** 形 輝く
- **shook** 動 shake (振る) の過去
- **shortly** 副 まもなく, すぐに
- **should have done** ～すべきだった (のにしなかった)《仮定法》
- **shoulder** 名 肩 take someone by the shoulders (人の) 両肩をつかむ
- **shovel** 名 シャベル
- **show ～ around** ～を案内して回る
- **show up** 顔を出す, 現れる
- **shown** 動 show (見せる) の過去分詞
- **shrink** 動 ①縮む, 縮小する ②尻込みする, ひるむ
- **shut** 動 ①閉まる, 閉める, 閉じる ②たたむ ③閉じ込める ④shutの過去, 過去分詞
- **side** 名 側, 横, そば, 斜面 from side to side 左右に
- **sight** 熟 in sight 視野に入って
- **silence** 名 沈黙, 無言, 静寂
- **silent** 形 ①無言の, 黙っている ②静かな, 音を立てない
- **silently** 副 静かに, 黙って
- **silver** 名 銀, 銀貨, 銀色 形 銀製の
- **simply** 副 ①簡単に ②単に, ただ ③まったく, 完全に
- **since** 熟 ever since それ以来ずっと
- **singer** 名 歌手, シンガー
- **single** 形 たった1つの
- **sink** 動 沈む, 沈める, 落ち込む
- **slap** 動 (平手, 平たいもので) ぴしゃりと打つ
- **sleep** 熟 go to sleep 寝る
- **slightly** 副 わずかに, いささか
- **slow down** 速度を落とす
- **slowly** 副 遅く, ゆっくり
- **smart** 形 ①利口な, 抜け目のない ②きちんとした, 洗練された
- **smile at** ～に微笑みかける
- **smoke** 動 喫煙する, 煙を出す 名 煙
- **smoking** 名 喫煙
- **so** 熟 and so そこで, それだから, それで or so ～かそこらで so many 非常に多くの so that ～するために, それで, ～できるように so ～ that … 非常に～なので… So what? それがどうした。どうでもいいではないか。
- **soap** 名 石けん
- **softly** 副 柔らかに, 優しく, そっと
- **soldier** 名 兵士, 兵卒
- **solid** 形 ①固体 [固形] の ②頑丈な ③信頼できる
- **some** 熟 for some reason なんらかの理由で, どういうわけか in some way 何とかして, 何らかの方法で some time いつか, そのうち some way しばらく
- **somebody** 代 誰か, ある人

- □ **somehow** 副 ①どうにかこうにか, ともかく, 何とかして ②どういうわけか
- □ **someone** 代 ある人, 誰か
- □ **something** 代 ①ある物, 何か ②いくぶん, 多少
- □ **sometime** 副 いつか, そのうち
- □ **sometimes** 副 時々, 時たま
- □ **somewhere** 副 ①どこかへ[に] ②いつか, およそ
- □ **soon** 熟 as soon as ～するとすぐ, ～するや否や sooner or later 遅かれ早かれ
- □ **sort** 名 種類, 品質 a sort of ～のようなもの, 一種の～
- □ **South Sea** 南洋
- □ **speaking** 名 話すこと, 談話, 演説
- □ **speed off** (車が)飛び出す
- □ **speed up** 速度を上げる
- □ **sped** 動 speed (急ぐ)の過去, 過去分詞
- □ **spill** 動 こぼす, まき散らす
- □ **spot** 名 ①地点, 場所, 立場 ②斑点, しみ
- □ **spy** 名 スパイ
- □ **stair** 名 ①(階段の)1段 ②《-s》階段, はしご
- □ **stand up** 立ち上がる
- □ **stare** 動 じっと[じろじろ]見る stare out ～をじっと見つめる
- □ **statement** 名 声明, 述べること
- □ **stay on top of** ～を完全に掌握している
- □ **steal** 動 盗む
- □ **step out** 外へ出る
- □ **stick out** 突き出す
- □ **sticky** 形 ①くっつく, 粘着性の ②蒸苦しい ③やっかいな
- □ **stiff** 形 ①堅い, 頑固な ②堅苦しい get stiff 硬直する
- □ **stir** 動 動かす, かき回す stir up 荒立てる, 引き起こす
- □ **stock** 名 株式
- □ **stockbroker** 名 株式仲買人
- □ **stomach** 名 ①胃, 腹 ②食欲, 欲望, 好み
- □ **storm** 名 嵐, 暴風雨
- □ **straighten** 動 まっすぐにする[なる] straighten up 背筋をしゃんと伸ばす
- □ **strangely** 副 奇妙に, 変に, 不思議なことに, 不慣れに
- □ **stream** 動 流れ出る, 流れる, なびく
- □ **stretch** 動 引き伸ばす, 広がる, 広げる stretch out ①手足を伸ばす, 背伸びする ②広がる
- □ **string** 名 ①ひも, 糸, 弦 ②一連, 一続き
- □ **stuck** 動 stick (刺さる)の過去, 過去分詞
- □ **stylish** 形 流行の, スタイリッシュな
- □ **subject** 熟 drop the subject 話題を打ち切る
- □ **success** 名 成功, 幸運, 上首尾
- □ **successful** 形 成功した, うまくいった
- □ **such ~ that ...** 非常に～なので…
- □ **such a** そのような
- □ **sudden** 形 突然の, 急な all of a sudden 突然, 前触れもなしに
- □ **suffer** 動 ①(苦痛・損害などを)受ける, 苦しむ, 悩む
- □ **suit** 名 スーツ, 背広

- **suitable** 形 適当な, 似合う, ふさわしい
- **sunset** 名 日没, 夕焼け
- **Superior** 名 《Lake –》スペリオル湖
- **supper** 名 夕食, 晩さん, 夕飯
- **suppose** 動 ①仮定する, 推測する ②《be -d to ~》～することになっている, ～するものである
- **sure** 熟 make sure 確かめる, 確認する
- **surprised** 形 驚いた be surprised at ～に驚く be surprised to do ～して驚く
- **surrender** 動 降服する
- **surround** 動 囲む, 包囲する
- **swimmer** 名 泳ぐ人, 水泳選手
- **swimming** 名 水泳
- **swing** 動 ①揺り動かす, 揺れる ②回転する, ぐるっと回す
- **swore** 動 swear（誓う）の過去

T

- **T. J. Eckleburg** T・J・エクルバーグ《人名》
- **take** 熟 It takes someone ~ to … (人)が…するのに～(時間など)がかかる It takes two people to ~するには2人必要 take a walk 散歩をする take away ①連れ去る ②取り上げる, 奪い去る ③取り除く take back ①取り戻す ②(言葉, 約束を)取り消す, 撤回する take into 手につかむ, 中に取り入れる take on (性質を)帯びる, 獲得する take one's eyes off ～から目をそらす take out 取り出す, 取り外す, 連れ出す, 持って帰る take over 引き継ぐ, 支配する, 乗っ取る take someone aside (人)をわきへ呼ぶ take someone away (人)を連れ出す take someone by the shoulders (人の)両肩をつかむ take up 取り上げる, 拾い上げる, やり始める, (時間・場所を)とる take ~ to … ~を…に連れて行く
- **taste** 名 ①味, 風味 ②好み, 趣味
- **taxi** 名 タクシー
- **tender** 形 柔らかい, 優しい
- **tent** 名 テント, 天幕
- **territory** 名 ①領土 ②(広い)地域, 範囲, 領域
- **terror** 名 ①恐怖 ②恐ろしい人[物]
- **thank ~ for** ～に対して礼を言う
- **that** 熟 after that その後 now that 今や～だから, ～からには so that ～するために, それで, ～できるように so ~ that … 非常に～なので… such ~ that … 非常に～なので… this and that あれやこれや That's all right. いいんですよ。
- **theater** 名 劇場
- **then** 熟 just then そのとたんに then and there その場ですぐに
- **there** 熟 here and there あちこちで over there あそこに then and there その場ですぐに there comes a point ～になることがある up there あそこに
- **these days** このごろ
- **thick** 形 厚い, 密集した, 濃厚な
- **thin** 形 薄い, 細い, やせた out of thin air どこからともなく
- **think of** ～のことを考える, ～を思いつく, 考え出す
- **Third Division** 第3師団
- **this** 熟 in this way このようにして

- this and that あれやこれや　this one これ, こちら
- **those** 熟 in those days あのころは, 当時は
- **though** 接 ①〜にもかかわらず, 〜だが ②たとえ〜でも　as though あたかも〜のように, まるで〜みたいに　even though 〜であるけれども, 〜にもかかわらず　副 しかし
- **throat** 名 のど, 気管
- **throughout** 前 ①〜中, 〜を通じて ②〜のいたるところに
- **throw a party** パーティーを開く
- **throw down** 投げ出す, 放棄する
- **time** 熟 all the time ずっと, いつも, その間ずっと　any time いつでも　at the time そのころ, 当時は　by the time 〜する時までに　each time 〜するたびに　every time 〜するときはいつも　some time いつか, そのうち
- **tiny** 形 ちっぽけな, とても小さい
- **tired** 形 ①疲れた, くたびれた ②あきた, うんざりした　be tired of 〜に飽きて[うんざりして]いる
- **Tom Buchanan** トム・ブキャナン《人名》
- **too much of** あまりに〜過ぎる
- **top** 熟 stay on top of 〜を完全に掌握している　with the top down (車の)トップを下ろして
- **tore** 動 tear (裂く)の過去
- **total** 動 合計する
- **tournament** 名 トーナメント
- **towel** 名 タオル
- **trace** 動 たどる, さかのぼって調べる
- **tradition** 名 伝統, 伝説, しきたり
- **trail** 動 ひきずる, 跡を追う　trail off (音声が)次第に小さくなる
- **train car** (列車の)車両
- **tray** 名 盆, 盛り皿
- **trial** 名 裁判
- **trick** 名 策略, 手品　動 だます
- **truck** 名 トラック, 運搬車
- **truly** 副 本当に
- **trust** 動 信用[信頼]する
- **truth** 名 真理, 事実, 本当
- **try on** 試着してみる
- **turn** 熟 be turned away 追い返される　turn around 振り向く, 向きを変える, 方向転換する　turn away 向こうへ行く, 追い払う, (顔を)そむける, 横を向く　turn back 元に戻る　turn in 向きを変える, (向きを変えてわき道になどに)入る, 床につく　turn into 〜に変わる　turn off 〜を止める, (照明などを)消す　turn out (照明などを)消す　turn to 〜の方を向く

U

- **unbelievable** 形 信じられない(ほどの), 度のはずれた
- **unclear** 形 明確でない, はっきりしない
- **uncomfortable** 形 心地よくない
- **understanding** 名 理解　形 理解のある, 思いやりのある
- **uneasily** 副 不安気に, 不愉快に
- **uneasy** 形 不安な, 焦って
- **unhappily** 副 不幸に, 運悪く, 不愉快そうに
- **unhappy** 形 不運な, 不幸な
- **university** 名 (総合)大学
- **unpleasant** 形 不愉快な, 気にさわ

- □ **untrue** 形 真実でない, 事実に反する
- □ **unusual** 形 普通でない, 珍しい, 見[聞き]慣れない
- □ **up there** あそこで
- □ **upset** 形 憤慨して, 動揺して
- □ **upstairs** 副 2階へ[に], 階上へ 名 2階, 階上
- □ **used** 動 ①use（使う）の過去, 過去分詞 ②《– to》よく～したものだ, 以前は～であった 形 ①慣れている,《get [become] – to》～に慣れてくる ②使われた, 中古の
- □ **useless** 形 役に立たない, 無益な

V

- □ **valley** 名 谷, 谷間
- □ **visible** 形 目に見える, 明らかな

W

- □ **waiter** 名 ウェイター, 給仕
- □ **wake up** 起きる, 目を覚ます
- □ **walk** 熟 go for a walk 散歩に行く take a walk 散歩をする walk about 歩き回る walk ahead of ～の前を歩く walk along （前へ）歩く, ～に沿って歩く walk around 歩き回る, ぶらぶら歩く walk away 立ち去る, 遠ざかる walk on 歩き続ける walk out of ～から出る walk out the door ドアの外に出る, どこかに行く walk over ～の方に歩いていく walk past 通り過ぎる
- □ **wall** 熟 against the wall 壁を背にして
- □ **Walter Chase** ウォルター・チェイス《人名》
- □ **wander** 動 さまよう, 放浪する wander into 入り込む
- □ **warmly** 副 温かく, 親切に
- □ **warmth** 名 暖かさ, 思いやり
- □ **watch out for** ～に注意する
- □ **watch over** 見守る, 見張る
- □ **wave** 名 波 動 （手などを振って）合図する
- □ **way** 熟 in a way ある意味では in one way or another あれこれと, どうにかして in some way 何とかして, 何らかの方法で in this way このようにして make one's way 進む, 行く, 成功する make way 道を譲る[あける], 前進する on one's way to ～に行く途中で some way しばらく
- □ **wealth** 名 ①富, 財産 ②豊富, 多量
- □ **wealthy** 形 裕福な, 金持ちの
- □ **wedding** 名 結婚式, 婚礼
- □ **weekend** 熟 on (the) weekends 週末に
- □ **weep** 動 しくしく泣く, 嘆き悲しむ
- □ **weight** 名 重さ, 重力, 体重
- □ **West Indies** 《the –》西インド諸島
- □ **wet** 形 ぬれた, 湿った, 雨の
- □ **what** 熟 So what? それがどうした。どうでもいいではないか。 What about ～? ～についてあなたはどう思いますか。～はどうですか。 what if もし～だったらどうなるだろうか what … for どんな目的で What's the matter? どうしたんですか。
- □ **whatever** 代 ①《関係代名詞》～するものは何でも ②どんなこと[もの]が～とも 形 ①どんな～でも ②《否

- **wheel** 名《the-》ハンドル
- **whenever** 接 ①〜するときはいつでも、〜するたびに ②いつ〜しても
- **whether** 接 〜かどうか、〜かまたは…、〜であろうとなかろうと
- **while** 熟 after a while しばらくして for a while しばらくの間、少しの間
- **whiskey** 名 ウイスキー
- **whisper** 動 ささやく、小声で話す
- **white** 熟 dress in white 白い服を着る
- **white race** 白色人種
- **who** 熟 anybody who 〜する人はだれでも
- **whole** 形 全体の、すべての、完全な、満〜、丸〜
- **whom** 代 ①誰を[に] ②《関係代名詞》〜するところの人、そしてその人を
- **Why don't you ~?** 〜したらどうだい、〜しませんか。
- **Why not?** どうしてだめなのですか。いいですとも。ぜひそうしよう！
- **wide** 形 幅の広い、広範囲の、幅が〜ある
- **wildly** 副 荒々しく、乱暴に、むやみに
- **Wilson** 名 ウィルソン《人名》
- **wink** 動 ウインクする、まばたきする
- **wipe** 動 〜をふく、ぬぐう、ふきとる
- **wise** 形 賢明な、聡明な、博学の
- **witness** 名 ①証拠、証言 ②目撃者
- **wives** 名 wife (妻) の複数
- **woke** 動 wake (目が覚める) の過去
- **Wolfsheim** 名 ウォルフシェム《人名》
- **wonder** 動 ①不思議に思う、(〜に) 驚く ②(〜かしらと) 思う wonder about 〜について知りたがる wonder if 〜ではないかと思う 名 驚き(の念)、不思議なもの in wonder 驚いて
- **wooden** 形 木製の、木でできた
- **work on** 〜で働く、〜に取り組む、〜を説得する、〜に効く
- **world** 熟 all over the world 世界中に
- **worried** 動 worry (悩む) の過去、過去分詞 形 心配そうな、不安げな
- **worse** 副 いっそう悪く
- **worth** 形 (〜の) 価値がある、(〜) しがいがある 名 価値、値打ち
- **would** 熟 would have … if 〜 もし〜だったとしたら…しただろう would like 〜がほしい would like to 〜したいと思う would rather 〜する方がよい Would you like 〜? 〜はいかがですか。
- **write to** 〜に手紙を書く
- **writing** 名 筆跡
- **WWI** 略 第一次世界大戦

Y

- **yacht** 名 ヨット
- **Yale Club** イェールクラブ《会員制組織》
- **yawn** 動 あくびをする
- **yell** 動 大声をあげる、わめく
- **you** 熟 See you. ではまた。 you know ご存知のとおり、そうでしょう you see あのね、いいですか

やさしい英語を聴いて読む
IBCオーディオブックス

グレート・ギャツビー
The Great Gatsby
[新装版]

2016年11月7日　第1刷発行

原著者 ……… **F・スコット・フィッツジェラルド**

発行者 ……… **浦晋亮**

発行所 ……… **IBCパブリッシング株式会社**

〒162-0804
東京都新宿区中里町29番3号
菱秀神楽坂ビル9F
Tel. 03-3513-4511
Fax. 03-3513-4512
www.ibcpub.co.jp

印刷所 ……… **株式会社シナノパブリッシングプレス**

© IBC Publishing, Inc. 2016
Printed in Japan

カバーイラスト ……… **目黒 久美子**

落丁本・乱丁本は、小社宛にお送りください。
送料小社負担にてお取り替えいたします。
本書の無断複写(コピー)は
著作権法上での例外を除き禁じられています。

ISBN978-4-7946-0441-5

English Conversational Ability Test
国際英語会話能力検定

● **E-CATとは…**
英語が話せるようになるための
テストです。インターネットベー
スで、30分であなたの発話力を
チェックします。

www.ecatexam.com

● **iTEP®とは…**
世界各国の企業、政府機関、アメリカの大学300
校以上が、英語能力判定テストとして採用。オン
ラインによる90分のテストで文法、リーディング、
リスニング、ライティング、スピーキングの5技
能をスコア化。iTEP®は、留学、就職、海外赴任な
どに必要な、世界に通用する英語力を総合的に評
価する画期的なテストです。

www.itepexamjapan.com